The Heart of A Servant

THE HEART OF A SERVANT

With Hymns for Contemplation and Worship

DAVID E. ROSS
AND GARY A. PARRETT

XULON PRESS

Xulon Press
2301 Lucien Way #415
Maitland, FL 32751
407.339.4217
www.xulonpress.com

Paperback ISBN-13: 978-1-6628-5577-1
Ebook ISBN-13: 978-1-6628-5578-8

My child, give Me your heart,
and let your eyes delight in My ways.
Proverbs 23:26 (NRSV)

Here I am, Lord, take my heart
and let it become
a heart filled with Your love.
Henri Nouwen

Recommendations

"Thank you so much for writing this book! I gobbled it up as a famished child presented with delicious, nutritious foods! I look forward to reading it many more times.

I am sure as much as the professors and the 'sophisticated' appreciate what is written in the book, it is as much engaging for any child (or servant) of God. And for those who may have grown weary while ministering, it speaks like a loving parent, reminding the child, clarifying the wisdom of things above, while really knowing the child and where the child is coming from.

This book is unique, readers get two authors, their exchange, one expressing in prose, the other in poetry, giving us a fuller 'surround sound' on what it means to serve the glorious God of the Bible.

Those who wish to serve will be inspired by visions so right and beautiful.

Those who are serving now will sense the gentle guidance to do it right and well.

Those who have served and find themselves depleted and exhausted, will find understanding, restorative friends guiding them back to the joy of delighting in, and serving the One who fulfilled all righteousness."

Hyunmee Lee, Pianist, Mother, Music Minister,
many of whose recordings and PDFs are attached in Appendix 1

"David Ross is, in my opinion, one of the spiritual giants of our generation. The history of Christianity in Korea has forever been shaped by the ministry of both Ross and his wife, Ellen. The Heart of A Servant encapsulates the very best of their life's teaching. This volume, however, is more than a mere compendium of ideas. With the aid of Gary Parrett's catechetical hymns and musical accompaniments, the reader will discover many of the insights found in these pages modulated into worship! This book is a primer on how sound theology can and should lead to doxology. This volume warrants not only reading but careful rereading, meditation, and reflection on its life-forming and Godly wisdom. It is a tour de force of spiritual theology and Christian practice."

Chris Chun, Professor of Church History and Director of Jonathan Edwards Center at Gateway Seminary near Los Angeles, California

"The book is absolutely wonderful, and I love the way that your songs provide a worship and meditative response at the end of each chapter. It is a very beautiful offering and resource—Thank you so much for sharing it with us!!"

Julie Tennent, Church Musician and Hymnist , some of whose PDFs are attached in Appendix 1

"It is my honor to write a recommendation for this book as a leader of the Pneuma Springs community in Monroe, Washington. When I was asked to write a recommendation, I read this book in one sitting because it was so applicable to my situation. This book, The Heart of A Servant, is a must read for those who want to be a servant leader like Jesus Christ. This book is not for those who are ambitious and leaders who take the glory for themselves. Rather, this book is for humble leaders who are okay to be nameless leaders for the sake of giving glory to God.

The author, David Ross, has lived a life of a servant leader and continues to show us how to live as a servant leader. As the founder of YWAM Korea, he left for Korea 60 years ago as a Presbyterian missionary along with his wife Ellen. He spent twenty-five years in Korea and God brought them back to America to work with the Korean diasporas all over the world. I have known David for over thirty years now and I can surely say that he is a true servant of God. David's words are always rooted in the Bible, and he lives out the Word. Therefore, his words are powerful since he stands on the authority of God, and he is ready to obey God's will. David believes God's will in his life as a servant leader is to love everyone since we are beloved children of God. This book is a powerful book coming from a veteran missionary statesman, but it is more powerful because it is written from a life experience of the writer himself.

I have utmost respect for both David Ross and Gary Parrett. Gary is a walking miracle and God continues to show His goodness through Gary as he recovers from a tragic accident. I was tearing up as I was reading this book because of God's goodness in Gary's life. Gary has suffered a lot but reading this book gives me hope. It is my prayer that you will be blessed as you read this book as much as it has blessed me. If you are a Christ follower reading this book, this book will wake you up to live a real servant life as you strive to become like Him. Thank you David and Gary for being our inspiration both in writing and in real life."

Peter Yang, Director at Youth With A Mission (YWAM)
Antioch Institute for International Mission (AIIM)

"The Heart of A Servant is a significant book that in chorus uncovers fresh connections between building the House of the Lord and fulfilling the Great Commission. As the prophet Haggai stated, David Ross and Gary Parrett have given "careful thought" to uniting scriptures, life experiences, natural surroundings, and original hymns with musical accompaniments to honor God and edify the church to embrace the meaning of servanthood. I had the pleasure of serving alongside of David and Ellen Ross, Gary and Holly Parrett during the 1980s, in Korea and New York City respectively, where I learned the importance of listening and paying attention. However, after reading The Heart of A Servant I have come to understand more fully the depth of their life's mission to see servants planted in every nation endeavoring to change their communities and their world.

This book, however, is not only a timely word to all who desire to gain multiple aspects of servanthood, but also it is a timely word for all who want to go beyond "the statue in a garden" and recognize the importance of serving a broken world to see healing and peace transform our spiritual and natural environments. The Heart of A Servant is a vital work that not only encourages believers to become more committed to obeying God, but also a work that deserves rereading, all while meditating and reflecting on intimacy with God and community."

Mark M. Chambers teaches environmental history at Stony Brook University in New York, and is currently a Rita Allen Civic Science Fellow Researching Environmental Justice concerns.

Table of Contents

Preface. xv

A Word of Thanks xix

Introduction. xxi

Chapter 1. Enfolded in God's Love 1

Chapter 2. The Suffering Servant. 9

Chapter 3. The Suffering Servant Is Lord of All. 19

Chapter 4. The Servant's Power 26

Chapter 5. The Servant of Justice. 38

Chapter 6. The Servant of the Word 50

Chapter 7. The Servant of Love 66

Chapter 8. The Servant of Peace. 75

Chapter 9. The Servant's Community. 86

Chapter 10. The Hidden Servant. 99

Chapter 11. The Paradox of Servant Ministry 113

Chapter 12. The Servant in the World. 124

Chapter 13. The Servant's Call. 133

David's Final Word to Servants 141

Gary's Final Word to Servants 143

Preface

"Let the word of Christ dwell in you richly as you teach and admonish one another with all wisdom, and as you sing psalms, hymns and spiritual songs with gratitude in your hearts to God" (Col. 3:16).

"Instead, be filled with the Spirit. Speak to one another with psalms, hymns and spiritual songs. Sing and make music in your hearts to the Lord..." (Eph. 5:18-19).

Worship should be both God-honoring and church-edifying. How does Christian worship actually form its participants? The rhythm of revelation and response gives shape to our lives (Is. 6:1-13; cf. Rom. 12:1-2). As we worship, God's Person, work and will are revealed among us in greater measure, and we are called toward more faithful response at each point.

As I was reading David's meditations, the songs for each chapter often just arose in my heart from among the hundreds of songs & hymns I have fully or partially composed. It was as if my heart was responding with songs to the revealed truth in David's Biblical teachings. There is a powerful link between biblical teaching and hymn singing, and this is a connection Holly and I have very often enjoyed with David and Ellen. We have been truly blessed by their spiritual teaching, and they have been among the most persistent lovers of our songs. Through this small and imperfect part I can contribute to David's book, it is my prayer that worship of our God, the rhythm of

God's revelation and our response would become a part of who we are as servants of the Almighty and living God.

My wife Holly and I have truly been blessed by David and Ellen Ross ever since we first met them in 1985 while ministering in New York City. We have often had the privilege of ministering together with them, especially among Korean Americans, and have learned shepherding skills from these wiser and more experienced servant-leaders. As I write this preface now, however, I stand more as a grateful recipient of the faithful servants who embraced and shepherded me again and again, often through the hardest times.

In 2010, I survived a deadly airport bus accident in Korea on my way to Sri Lanka after a week of teaching in Korea. This accident killed 14 people instantly, including our dear friend, Pastor Kenny Ye. I sustained a severe Traumatic Brain Injury (TBI) and was in a coma for 10 weeks after the accident. This injury took away much of my ability to minister as I used to. Along with physical and mobility impairment, my thinking, speaking, teaching and writing all have been affected. About 18 months after the accident I went through a mental breakdown as I struggled with what had been stripped off and what I was left with to face. During the last 11 years and through all of my still ongoing recovery, David & Ellen have been powerful servants for me and my family. They were not only there for us through prayers but also with willingness to serve us in every crisis we faced, in tangible, practical and spiritual ways. They called us to Kona to be with them and the YWAM Disciple Training School when I was going through a mental breakdown. My wife Holly and I received so much healing through their love, generosity, and spiritual ministry. I can't even count the numerous times they have risen to stand with and help us through. They, over and over, modeled and offered Jesus' grace and servant hearts.

I also see this invitation to be a part of this book project as David's service and ministry to me. David, though very aware of my loss and limitations from the brain injury, trusted God and me to be a part of this important project. Even in my small participation, I have had to depend constantly upon his patient and humble servant heart towards me and am exceedingly grateful.

The content of this book does not come from head knowledge but from David's and Ellen's servant hearts that have been faithfully lived out through their life and ministry. We are living witnesses and grateful benefactors of these servants of God, and we will be blessed and do well to heed and follow the way these servants have served God and His people.

Learning to be servants of the Lord Jesus,
Gary and Holly Parrett

You can find all of Gary's songs in Appendix 1 on my YouTube channel (gap2Theos) in the playlist linked here: *https://tinyurl.com/ theheartofaservant*

A Word of Thanks

"Behold, how good and pleasant it is when brothers and sisters dwell in unity! For there the Lord has commanded the blessing, life forevermore" (Ps. 133:1,3).

This abundant life is the Good Shepherd's gift to us, to be shared with Him but also with our brothers and sisters in Christ throughout the world. This life is so rich and beautiful that we must sing it, both to God and also to one another, in order to appreciate its depth and beauty. We are created to worship God. Gary Parrett expressed it well when he said that "the rhythm of revelation and response gives shape to our lives."

Our great desire is that this book will express this rhythm of revelation and response through the combination of receiving God's revelation of what it means to be a servant of the Lord and responding in hymns for contemplation and worship. When we sing the hymns of praise and worship after each teaching, God reveals Himself to us in greater measure, and we will discover that the Holy Spirit is reshaping our lives to conform to Jesus Christ, our Savior, who chose to come as the Suffering Servant.

It is a special blessing to be able to minister with Gary Parrett in making this book available to our brothers and sisters throughout the world. When I listen to Gary's hymns, I am reminded of the words of another hymn writer. Martin Luther wrote in 1523 that he penned hymns "so that the Word of God may be among the people in the form of music" (Plough Quarterly, Spring 2022, p. 79). This is our hope for you, the readers. Ellen and I have shared a beautiful friendship with Gary and Holly for many years, and they have been our spiritual mentors as well as friends. As I listen and sing these beautiful hymns and read Gary and Holly's interpretations, I am discovering a new depth of wisdom and strength that God has given Gary in his weakness. Only the Lord knows how many people have been blessed through their love and wisdom.

We have remembered all of you, our dear friends and fellow servants, and prayed prayers of thanksgiving to God for you while preparing this book. You have blessed and enriched our lives far more than we deserve or could have imagined. May God's fruit continue to abound as you serve Him with joy in this critical time.

Thank you, Debbie, Becky and Judy for making this book better by your excellent proofreading. Thank you, Seong Bo Kim, for making this book richer through your wonderful translation into the Korean language.

To God be all the glory.
David and Ellen Ross

Remember! It is important to meditate and listen to Gary's hymns at the end of each chapter. They lead us into worship by singing the same truths that have been spoken in each chapter. You will be able to listen to each hymn by referring to Appendix 1. True theology (understanding God and His truth) leads into doxology (praising God).

Introduction

The Spirit of God is moving throughout the world today, searching for people whose hearts belong fully to God. When He finds such a person, He strengthens her/him greatly by filling her with God's love and power. He then calls that person to become His servant, to change the world.

Before you say, "Oh, that leaves me out, I'm not a pastor or a missionary," remember: the Bible does not use the word "servant" to signify a special category of Christians; nor is it a professional title or radical name given to one who goes to live in a danger zone, although some servants are called to do so.

The truth is, we already are servants. We all are slaves, which is another meaning of the word *doulos* in the New Testament. We may be slaves of money, of power, or sex or social position. These are the idols, or gods, of today's world. These gods are controlled by the god of this world, whose name is Satan. But Jesus Christ came into the world to destroy the works of the devil (1 Jn. 3:8)! He completed this work by becoming a servant, not of the devil but of God. He suffered and died on the cross, and rose again to free us from Satan's control; we are no longer slaves, or servants of sin and the devil. We now are free to become Jesus' servants.

The great value of our work as servants is not the work, or the serving, itself. What matters is that our service is the service *of God.*

What will happen if we decide to become a servant of the Lord? What does it mean? The purpose of this book is to help readers understand what the Bible means when God calls us to be His servants. How does a servant live in this modern world? What are the blessings that come to a church that commits to serving the world as God did in Jesus Christ? How can I become God's instrument to help the Church worldwide become God's servant church?

These and other questions will be answered as we examine the life of Jesus Christ, the Suffering Servant, as well as the lives of other servants whom God has used to change the world.

Chapter One

Enfolded in God's Love

One who trusts in Yahweh is enfolded in His faithful love.
Ps. 32:10 (NJB)

T he apostle Paul revealed his true identity in the opening words of his Letter to the Romans: "Paul, a servant of Christ Jesus." He had many functions; apostle, teacher, missionary, theologian. But none of these defined him. He had only one identity in the ministry to which God called him: servant of Christ Jesus.

It was the identity he chose on the Road to Damascus when he asked the Lord, "What shall I do, Lord?" (Acts 22:10 NASB). The moment he met the Risen Lord, he was born again and became a son of God. This became his family identity. His question revealed his ministry identity: What would you have me do, Lord? A child of God can ask no greater question.

God's *Poiema*

Paul wrote to the Christians in Ephesus and reminded them that they were God's *poiema* (poem, His workmanship, masterpiece), "created in Christ Jesus for good works, which God prepared beforehand, that we should walk in them" (Eph. 2:10).

1

Gary Parrett's beautiful song and clear description of the Church as God's *poiema* (included at the end of this chapter) helps us understand what it means to be a servant Church. He reminds us that while each of us is uniquely created and formed by God's handiwork (Ps. 139), we are together the *poiema* of God, His work of art, His masterpiece. God's purpose in creating us was that we might do the "good works" which God has already designated to make up our way of life.

God wants us individually, and even more importantly corporately, as His servant Church, to be a part of His great plan to unite all things in Jesus Christ, so that His Kingdom may come, and His will be done on earth as it is in heaven. Jesus Christ invites us to become His servants, with His guarantee that we will be enfolded in His love as we love the world as He does.

The Meaning of Servant

The Bible defines a servant of the Lord in two ways.

First, a servant is one who belongs to God. "I have called you by name, you are Mine" (Is. 43:1 NASB). We are "owned" by God, His precious possession. He loves us unconditionally, cherishes and honors us, protects us, guards us, enjoys us and continually renews us in His love. He even dances over us with shouts of joy, as if each day were a festival (Zeph. 3:17)! The psalmist describes it best when he says that God's servants are "enfolded in His faithful love" (Ps. 32:10 NJB).

God calls us into a covenant relationship, just as He called Abraham (Gen. 12:1-3). A covenant relationship includes promise and command. God's promise is that "goodness and mercy shall follow me all the days of my life" (Ps. 23:6). The word "mercy" in Hebrew is *hesed,* God's steadfast love, faithful love, unfailing love. His love is always available and never runs out, and it will pursue me all the days of my life. It is His active love that never fails to transform His servants into the image of His Son, Jesus Christ. Only a servant can understand Jesus' promise in John 10:10 – "I came that they may have life and have it abundantly." Great is the Lord, who delights in the welfare of His servant (Ps. 35:27)! God's command is that we obey Him without condition. Covenant life in Christ becomes complete when we respond to God through the loving obedience of our faith.

Hans Uhrs von Balthasar, in his book *Prayer,* which has transformed the prayer life of many Christians, including my own, reminds us that we participate in God's divine nature (2 Pet. 1:3-4). When the apostle John said that which we have heard, which we seen with our eyes and have touched with our hands, concerning the word of life (1 John 1:1)—Jesus Christ, he was not speaking only of the original disciples of the Lord, but was including all of us who are His disciples today. God has "opened His inner life" to His servants. His Holy Spirit continues to "enlighten the eyes of our heart" (Eph. 1:18) so that we can see Christ; we can hear and touch the "Word of life" of the triune God just as His original followers did. The great fruit of our prayer life is that God unfolds this "faith-knowledge" of "seeing, hearing and touching" as we seek to know and trust the Lord more. When God became a man in Jesus Christ, His purpose was "that God's inner nature and life should be opened to us, should become familiar to us, and that we should experience with our very being, and hence also with our minds and senses, what it means to say that *God is love"* (*Prayer,* Hans Uhrs von Balthasar, Ignatius Press, 1986. pp. 177-182).

A servant of God knows and experiences the height and depth, the length and breadth of God's love. This is the love of God the Trinity— Father, Son and Holy Spirit; one member of the Trinity became a man and revealed this love to the world. Even nominal Christians know God's love, because they have received it as a gift. But only the servant of the Lord understands that everything begins with the love of God. God loves the world, and He calls everyone who loves Him to become His servant to share His love with the world. This leads us to the second meaning of a servant of the Lord.

Second, a servant is one who stands under the authority of God, ready to obey His will. "You are My servant ... in whom I will be glorified" (Is. 49:3). Just as God loves us completely, without conditions, so we, His servants, obey God, without conditions. We renounce our own will, including our opinions and ideas, so that by obedience we may offer Him our love.

The life of a servant of Jesus Christ is all about love. The servant hears God say, "You are My beloved child, My beloved servant." We surrender our own free will in loving obedience to God, and by doing so the whole concept of "servant and master" is transformed. Being a servant of God can in no way be compared to the indignity of the human servant-master relationship.

We follow in the steps of the Suffering Servant, Jesus Christ, who prayed in His hour of crisis that the Father's will, not His own, might be done. He did this because He loved His Father and delighted to do His will. He abandoned His own will, plans and ideas, so that His Father's perfect will could be accomplished. Servants eagerly wait to do God's will, always listening in order to obey. The sacrifice servants give to God is that of spiritual worship, offering to God their bodies as a living sacrifice. God is pleased with His servants' loving obedience.

Beginning to Live As Servants

It is not easy to become a servant of the Lord. Only when we are overwhelmed by the Father's unconditional love for us, and when we give our love fully to Him, can we respond to Jesus' call to become His servant. Servants begin by loving God; but we know that the proof that we love God is our love for one another, just as Christ has loved us (Jn. 13:34-35). "By this we know love, that he laid down His life for us, and we ought to lay down our lives for the brothers" (1 Jn. 3:16). Throughout history, the world has immediately recognized the servant church. "Behold, how these Christians love one another!"

But a servant Church does not stop with loving one another. God continually enlarges His servants' vision. He spoke to His people of Israel when they were returning from long years of exile. They were eager to work together to heal the division that had taken place in their nation between south and north. But God says, "It is too light a thing that you should be My servant [to heal the wounds of your own nation]; I will make you a light for the nations, that My salvation may reach to the end of the earth" (Is. 49:6)!

The servant Church obeys God's command to invite the world to share this Good News that they also can meet God, can see and touch the Word of Life. Von Balthasar speaks in his book on prayer about the urgency of evangelism and our mission to the world. He maintains that the Christian Church "owes it to the world" to give the world a clear understanding that, although the Spirit of God awakens spiritual hunger in people of every race, creed, and nation, His witness is to only one Redeemer, who is the Word of life, Christ Jesus the Lord.

God's last word to the world is Jesus Christ (Heb. 1:1-2). He is the great Suffering Servant who has called us to become His servants. He empowers us to serve the world as He did, and to invite all people to welcome His loving embrace.

Hymn for Contemplation and Worship

His POIEMA! (Ephesians)

Praise Jesus for God's glorious grace.
For us He left His high and holy place.
On earth will we reflect His face.
We are the workmanship of God! (Eph.1:1-2:10)

One Body of our risen Lord.
By grace through faith we are saved by the Word;
created new to do good works. (2:10)
We are the boasting of our God! (2:10-22)

Intercede from Him and for Him.
We pray His greater victories to win.
We share God's truth; we sing His hymns.
We are the poem of our God! (3:1-21)

Edify for His Body's health,
equip the pilgrims with God's greater wealth,
our Lord ascended sends forth help.
We are the handiwork of God! (4:1-32)

Maturing words when we are weak:
Psalms, hymns and spiritual songs we will speak.
Wonder we are; wonder we seek:
Spirit-filled Masterpiece of God! (5:1-6:9)

Armor we wear, when called to war.
Salvation's helmet now the Church adorns.
Our shield is faith, God's Word our sword.
We are His POIEMA! Amen. (6:10-24)

"For it is by grace you (plural you) have been saved, through faith – and this not from yourselves, it is the gift of God – not by works, so that no one can boast. For we are God's **workmanship, (boasting), (poem), (handiwork), (masterpiece)**; we are His **POIEMA!**, created in Christ Jesus to do good works, which God prepared in advance for us to do" Ephesians 2:8-10 (NIV).

I have written this hymn for the 300th Anniversary of the First Congregational Church of Hamilton, Massachusetts. It was my prayer and encouragement to one of the oldest congregations in America to continue being the POIEMA of God to the world. The hymn presents an acronym of POIEMA, the Greek word only found in Ephesians 2:10. Each of the verses presents a message from the book of Ephesians. In the hymn the underlined words are the suggested translations of POIEMA; the **bold** words represent my acronym of POIEMA.

The hymn works out as follows:
PRAISE refers to Eph. 1-2:10;
ONE BODY is the message of Eph. 2:10-22;
INTERCESSION (prayer) is the third part (Eph. 3);
EDIFICATION (building up-Eph. 4) leads to
MATURITY which is the focus from 5:1-6:9;
ARMOR which is the focus of 6:10-24.

The book of Ephesians is known as the book that shows how the church of Christ is to be to the world. NT Wright says in his book The Case for Psalms: "Paul speaks at one point of Christians as 'God's poem, God's 'artwork.' 'We are his 'workmanship,' say some of the translations of Ephesians 2:10. The Greek word Paul uses there is **poiēma**, the very word from which the English word 'poem' is derived. God gives us these poems, the Psalms, as a gift, in order that through our praying and singing of them he may give us as a gift to his world. We are called to be living, breathing, praying, singing poems."

As David in the preceding chapter emphasizes, as servants of God, we are to be the poiema to the world. "Jesus Christ invites us to be His servants to be enfolded in His love as we love the world as He does."

Chapter Two

The Suffering Servant

He made Himself nothing, taking the form of a servant (Phil. 2:7).

Sixty years ago my wife and I were called by God as missionaries to the people of Korea, both North and South. Over the years, we have come to understand our calling to include challenging and enabling Koreans to become missionaries to other countries, and helping to equip them in their servant ministry to the world. We went first to serve them, but soon discovered we were being served by them; we continue to seek together how we can best serve the world.

What is Unique about Christianity?

We must begin with the question we hear most often, "What is unique about Christianity?" Many Christian thinkers answer that miracles make Christianity unique. But even though they are important, they always point to something greater that lies beyond them. Theologians may say that doctrine makes us unique; but doctrine alone cannot explain the uniqueness. Others point to prophecies that have been fulfilled, or to the way the Christian Church has enabled nations to escape poverty and become prosperous. None of these answers is sufficient.

I believe the answer lies in asking the question, "What does God wish to say to the world?" In ancient times, God spoke through His prophets in many ways; but at one specific time in history He spoke His final word to the world. His word was: Jesus, His Son (Heb. 1:1)! His word was actually an action that revealed God's majestic love for the world. The Word became a human being, lived and suffered to the degree that even his own followers could not recognize Him. He was crucified, killed on a cross. All great religions offer sacrifices to please their gods. But God became His own sacrifice; He became the Suffering Servant who took the sins, sorrows and sicknesses of the whole world upon Himself and died. But He rose again!

What makes Christianity unique among the religions of the world? The cross and resurrection!

The Four Suffering Servant Songs of Isaiah (Is. 42:1-4; 49:1-7; 50:4-9; 52:13-53:12)

700 years before Jesus was born, Isaiah the prophet spoke about the suffering, the cross and the resurrection of Jesus Christ! God revealed to this faithful servant His great mystery of salvation for the world. Here is God's announcement that all the people of Israel had waited for, and longed for, for hundreds of years. Your Messiah is coming; His Kingdom is near! Isaiah recorded this prophecy in the form of four songs that are called the "Suffering Servant Songs." They are called songs, and not just poems, or prophetic writings, because they bring good news that must be sung! God has freed those who suffered the long exile, and they will be returning home! God has freed them from their captivity.

As Christians we must sing these songs, and not merely read them. Why is this? Because as we read and meditate on these four songs, we are confronted with what H.R. Mackintosh called "the sheer miracle right at the center of our life." We find ourselves forgiven! We have experienced God Himself setting us free. We are free from bondage to Satan, free from sin, no longer condemned. How can we not sing? The psalmist sang it with these words: "Our soul has escaped as a bird out of the snare of the fowler; the snare is broken, and we have escaped!

Our help is in the name of the LORD, who made heaven and earth" (Ps. 124:7-8 NASB).

The Fourth Suffering Servant Song (Is. 52:13—53:12)

We begin with the fourth Suffering Servant Song. God wants all Israel to be His servants, but this last song points to one Spirit-anointed servant. Jesus applied it to Himself. He is the Anointed One, the promised Messiah, Christ the Lord; and He promised His Spirit to His disciples so that they might continue in His mission. We are among His disciples who are called to be His servants to fulfill His Great Commission. As we begin our study of what it means to be a servant of the Lord, what better place to begin than this song about Jesus, the Suffering Servant of God?

The people who first heard this servant song were shocked, for two reasons. First, the Messiah who will bring in the Kingdom of God is disfigured beyond recognition. No one could have conceived of a king who is disfigured more than any other human. The second reason people were shocked was that this king would be high and lifted up, exalted above the nations. Only disciples of Jesus Christ, the Messiah, understand this seeming paradox, for Isaiah is speaking about the cross and resurrection of Christ.

Resurrection Enables us to Understand the Cross.

Resurrection is mentioned before crucifixion. "Behold, my servant will prosper, He will be high and lifted up, and greatly exalted." Only then are we told that His appearance was marred beyond recognition, causing everyone to be astonished (Is. 52:13-14).

Why is the resurrection mentioned before the crucifixion? Because we can understand Jesus' crucifixion only after we have experienced the power of His resurrection. Paul the apostle stated that his one goal in life was to know Christ Jesus his Lord; first, to know the power of

His resurrection, and then to share in the fellowship of His sufferings (Phil. 3:10-11). Paul was called to give hope to the world, to show that Jesus defeated suffering and death, and to proclaim that anyone can have new life in the Resurrected Lord! But even Paul could not fully understand the suffering of the cross until he met the Risen Christ on the road to Damascus. He experienced the power of Christ's resurrection, and this power enabled him to understand the cross.

We are resurrection people, and "Hallelujah!" is our song. We know that Christ died for the sins of the world, but the proof of that victory is that Christ rose again from the dead! Our hope is not limited to this life on earth; Christ was raised, and we also will be raised to unending life in Him. This is the announcement; and this is the key to understanding one of the greatest passages in the Bible: Isaiah chapter 53.

The cross is the heart of the Christian Faith.

The cross is the heart of the Christian faith. Paul says, in Galatians 6:14, that he boasts of nothing but the cross, through which the world is dead to him and by which he has died to the world. We also have been crucified with Christ. We no longer live, but rather Christ lives in us. The life we live, we live by faith in the Son of God who loved us and laid down His life for us.

We have spoken of the theologian who is known as the "theologian on his knees," Hans Uhrs von Balthasar. He maintains that the uniqueness of Christianity is a deed that is the greatest act of love the world has ever known. It is the *Majesty of Absolute Love,* the cross and resurrection of Jesus Christ, God's only Son. Love alone is credible.

What happened on the cross?

This important passage tells us what actually happened on the cross of Calvary. The Son of God came as a servant; and not merely a servant, but as the great Suffering Servant who carried all the sorrows of the world upon Himself and bore the grief of every person who has ever lived. He was a man of sorrows, despised and rejected by the very people who had longed for His coming.

Isaiah speaks specifically about four things that happened on the cross: He was wounded for our transgressions, crushed for our iniquities, chastised for our peace, and beaten for our healing (Is. 53:5).

He was wounded for our transgressions. Our *transgressions* refer to the actual sins we commit in word and deed every day. Through His death on the cross, Christ offers forgiveness daily to all who will turn from their sins. Each morning He invites us into His presence, to bestow upon us His mercy and grace to help in time of need (Heb. 4:14-16).

He was crushed for our iniquities. Our *iniquities* are the heart of sin: pride, arrogance, rebellion, all found in the heart of every human. Jesus, the Suffering Servant, was totally crushed and disfigured, because he allowed the weight of the world's pride to crush Him for our salvation.

He was chastised for our peace. We have *peace* with God, because the punishment of the world was laid on Jesus. We are reconciled to God (Rom. 5:1). We now have perfect peace—*shalom shalom*—inner wholeness and a deep inner peace that the world cannot understand. (Is. 26:3) This was Jesus' parting gift to His disciples: "Peace I leave with you; My peace I give to you. Not as the world gives do I give to you. Let not your hearts be troubled, neither let them be afraid" (John 14:27 ESV).

By His stripes we are healed. We find healing in the cross of Calvary. Jesus once visited His disciple Peter's home, where He healed Peter's mother in-law of a fever. Matthew wrote about this in his gospel (Matt. 8:17), and referred to the promise in Isaiah 53. Jesus is the Healer. This does not mean that we will never have sickness or disease. But it does mean that we can pray with hope, to receive spiritual, mental, emotional,

13

and physical healing. Indeed we are commanded to pray for healing, in both the Old and New Testaments. We can pray with confidence and boldness, because Jesus completed our whole salvation on the cross.

The Greatness of Our Salvation

The greatness of our salvation! Spirit, soul, and body, all have been made new! As we begin our walk as servants of the Lord, we do so by abiding in the Suffering Servant, who equips us to be His servants by this great salvation. He has freed us from the burden of sin, and from the anxiety of trying to justify ourselves by means of success, money, power, fame or pleasure. No servant of the Lord is burdened by a meaningless existence. We have no fears, not even fear of death. Our souls are anchored in God, and we have confidence that we will never be separated from His love.

But our salvation is even greater. We are not only freed *from* these things; we are also freed *for* something greater. Freed to serve God and freed to serve other people, even to give our lives for others. This freedom raises us up to be more than we can imagine; we no longer have to live in unrelenting sorrow or anger. We have a new beginning. We have a new freedom that expands our vision and enlarges our heart. We are freed to love one another as Christ has loved us, and to love the world sacrificially.

We are now called to be servants of the Kingdom of God, greatly loved by Him and blessed to be His agents for reconciliation. We are servants who have a restored relationship with God, in Jesus Christ. We are free servants; free from the guilt and power of sin. We have a new heart, and we are ready to serve the world in love.

Why not go into the world with a song in your heart? The joy of His salvation as your banner and the power of His Spirit as your strength? The promises of God as your confidence? "Fear not, for I am with you. Be not dismayed, for I am your God. I will strengthen you, I will help you. I will uphold you with My righteous right hand" (Is. 41:10).

Hymn for Contemplation and Worship

The Righteous One
Ps. 40:6-8; Heb. 10:1-25; Isa. 24:16, 53:11; Jer. 33:14-16; Acts 3:14; 7:52; 22:14; 1 Jn.2:1

When He came into the world,
heaven heard our Savior say:
"It was not for sacrifice
You have brought me to this day.
You prepared for me a body*,
I delight to do your will.
In the Scroll, my life is written;
Ev'ry word I will fulfill."

Chorus: Hallelujah!
Glory to the Righteous One.

In the Law was His delight,
ev'ry night and ev'ry day.
Ev'ry precept, at each point,
He did faithfully obey.
He was tempted just as we are,
but to sin He did not bow.
Sons of Adam, bruised and broken,
lift your eyes to this One now.

Chorus

Did the angels bow their heads?
Were the hosts of heaven hushed
when the One who knew no sin
became sin and curse for us?

For it pleased the LORD to crush Him.
Once for all the Just One died.
By His knowledge the LORD's Servant
has so many justified.

<u>Chorus</u>

In the tomb His body lay
when His perfect work was done.
But the doors of death gave way
to the risen Righteous One!
He ascended to the heavens,
with the Father now to reign.
Soon for judgment shall the Just One
come in glory once again.

//: **<u>Chorus</u>** (2x)

He who is our righteousness
calls us now to flee from sin.
But if any miss the mark
we must lift our eyes to Him.
Unto Jesus Christ the Righteous.
His blood speaks a better word.
He is ever interceding,
and His pleas for us are heard.

Soon the gates shall be flung open
to the ransomed of the Lord.
Soon the good and Faithful Servant
shall receive a just reward.
Soon the Zion-born shall be fully formed
to reflect their wondrous King.

Soon from ev'ry land lifting holy hands,
all the saints of God will sing ...

Chorus(2X): Hallelujah!
Glory to the Righteous One.

Hallelujah! Glory to the Righteous One who through His suffering and death has freed us from the bondage of sin and death, so that we can be "servants of the Kingdom of God, greatly loved by Him and blessed to be His agents for reconciliation. We are servants who have a restored relationship with God, in Jesus Christ. We are free servants; free from the guilt and power of sin. We have a new heart, and we are ready to serve the world in love." (David Ross)

As it is written: "There is no one righteous, not even one; there is no one who understands; there is no one who seeks God. All have turned away, they have together become worthless; there is no one who does good, not even one." Rom. 3:10-12

"But He was pierced for our transgressions, He was crushed for our iniquities; the punishment that brought us peace was on Him and by His wounds we are healed." Is. 53:5

"Out of the anguish of his soul he shall see and be satisfied; by his knowledge shall the Righteous One, my servant, make many to be accounted righteous, and he shall bear their iniquities." Is. 53:11

"From the ends of the earth we hear songs of praise, of glory to the Righteous One. But I say, 'I waste away, I waste away. Woe is me! For the traitors have betrayed, with betrayal the traitors have betrayed.'" Is. 24:16

Rev. 7:9-14 – "After this I looked, and behold, a great multitude that no one could number, from every nation, from all tribes and peoples and languages, standing before the throne and before the Lamb, clothed in white robes, with palm branches in their hands, and crying out with a loud voice, 'Salvation belongs to our God who sits on the throne, and to the Lamb!' And all the angels were standing around the throne and around the elders and the four living creatures, and they fell on their faces before the throne and worshiped God, saying, 'Amen! Blessing and glory and wisdom and thanksgiving and honor and power and might be to our God forever and ever! Amen.' Then one of the elders addressed me, saying, 'Who are these, clothed in white robes, and from where have they come?' I said to him, 'Sir, you know.' And he said to me, 'These are the ones coming out of the great tribulation. They have washed their robes and made them white in the blood of the Lamb.'"

Chapter Three

The Suffering Servant Is Lord of All

God has bestowed on Him the name that is above every name
(Phil. 2:9).

C hristians are people with a "song in their heart." The song is
one of praise to God for the majestic glory of His love. Who is
like the Lord our God, who is enthroned on high, yet loves the world
so much that He sacrificed His Son on the cross to deliver us from sin,
sorrows and sickness? We sing with joy because Jesus rose from the
dead and destroyed the works of the devil, who had the power of death.
The Suffering Servant is Lord of all! He now calls us to become His
servants of love to proclaim the Good News of His Kingdom.

The prophet Isaiah has revealed the depth of the Servant's suffering and the greatness of our salvation. Now the apostle Paul will
reveal the glory of the Risen Lord. Nowhere in all of Paul's writings
does he reach the beauty in expression of God's love in Jesus Christ
as he does in Philippians 2:5-11. He begins with Christ's pre-existence,
then speaks of His incarnation and death on the cross; he moves then
to His resurrection and ascension into heaven, and concludes with His
Lordship over all creation. This is the song Christians sing, but which
no other religion would dare to sing. This is the Lord who is calling us
to become His servants to the world.

This hymn of praise has two parts. The first part sings of Christ's humiliation (Phil. 2:5-8); the second part sings of God's exaltation of Jesus as King of kings and Lord of lords (Phil. 2:9-11).

The Mindset of a Christian – Gentleness and Humility

We must remember that Paul wrote this letter to the church he loved the most; they were his partners in mission. There was a problem of dissension in the Philippian church, and Paul gave them the key to unity by telling them they must have the mindset of Jesus, the Lord of the church. He began by telling them Christ was equal with God, but He humbled Himself and sacrificed Himself to become a human being. He went even further; although He was equal with God, He poured Himself out for the sake of sinful human beings by becoming a slave for the sake of those He loved and dying a scandalous death for the world!

This is the mindset every Christian must have. We are created in God's image, and the Holy Spirit works in each of us to restore that image and remold us into the character of Christ. To be made in God's image means to have the same mindset of Christ. Jesus Himself spoke of His character when He gave the great invitation to come to Him and find rest. "For I am gentle and lowly in heart, and you will find rest for your souls" (Matt. 11:29). Gentleness and humility are the two key marks of all servants of God. Gentleness, or meekness, means to yield in complete obedience to God, with joy; to have no will other than God's will. Humility means to lower ourselves, to empty ourselves so that we are nothing without God, that He may fill us with His fullness. We become able to love the world as God loves the world, and to express that love by sacrificing ourselves and becoming a servant (or slave) for the sake of others. Paul was telling his beloved Philippian Christians that if they would become servants, or slaves, first by loving one another and then by loving the world, there would be no dissension in the church.

Jesus alone was able to "explain" God (Jn 1:18–*exegesato:* to explain; make known). He revealed the truth that God is love and that love means self-sacrifice for the sake of others. Jesus revealed this truth not only by teaching about it but by actually becoming that self-sacrifice. He is the one whom John the Baptist introduced by saying, "Behold, the Lamb of God, who takes away the sin of the world" (Jn. 1:29)!

Gordon D. Fee, in his excellent commentary on Paul's Letter to the Philippians, reminds us that no one in Philippi, nor anywhere else in the Early Church, used the cross as a symbol of their faith. They did not put steeples with crosses on top of their churches, or wear a cross as a pendant or necklace. The cross was the greatest scandal, and it contradicted the world's human wisdom and power. Jesus, the Lord, was crucified as a criminal! The long awaited Messiah, the Christ, died on a cross! The symbol of the Early Church was the fish. *Ichthus,* the most commonly used Greek word for fish, contains the first letters of the following words: "Jesus Christ, Son of God, Savior." During times of persecution, Christians would often identify themselves to other Christians by drawing an outline of a fish in the sand.

God calls us today to become His servants to change the world. He gives us the "gift" that may not seem at first to be a gift, but which will enable us to change the world. "For it has been granted to you that for the sake of Christ you should not only believe in Him but also suffer for His sake" (Phil. 1:29). We enter into the fellowship of Christ's own sufferings for the world.

The Name Above Every Name

God acknowledges His Suffering Servant as Lord of all! He "exalted Him and bestowed on Him the name that is above every name" (Phil. 2:9-11). What is the name? LORD! God had spoken hundreds of years before through His servant Isaiah, and said: "There is no other god besides Me ... for I am God, and there is no other ... to me every knee shall bow, every tongue shall swear allegiance. Only in the Lord, it shall be said of Me, are righteousness and strength" (Is. 45:21-24).

What is the name? In Hebrew it is Yahweh (YHWH); translated into Greek it is LORD. God revealed His name to Moses as "I AM." There is no other being who can be called by this name. God is not merely rewarding Jesus because of His suffering and death; He is acknowledging that Jesus is Lord, that the name "LORD" has always belonged to His Son. "I AM" is Jesus' name. God—Father, Son and Holy Spirit—is I AM.

At the time Jesus was crucified, there were many "lords". Of course Caesar was considered to be the lord of all. When Paul wrote these words he was a prisoner of the emperor, and the Philippians were suffering because of this human lord. But God led Paul to announce to the world that there is only one true Lord, and that "at the name of Jesus every knee should bow, in heaven and on earth and under the earth, and every tongue confess that Jesus Christ is Lord, to the glory of God the Father" (Phil. 2:10-11).

Isaiah declared that God alone is Lord of all. Paul now quotes Isaiah, but uses the name "Jesus" for Lord! At the end of history, every person will bow his knee to Jesus Christ, the Lord of history. This does not mean that everyone will be saved. It does mean that the whole world will acknowledge Jesus Christ as Lord. Those in heaven are all the heavenly beings, both God's angels and Satan's demons. Those on earth are all humans living at the time of Jesus' return. Those under the earth probably refers to those who have died, but who will be raised first to greet the Lord at His return. When Peter preached his first sermon at Pentecost, he said these words: "Let all the house of Israel therefore know for certain that God has made Him both Lord and Christ, this Jesus whom you have crucified" (Acts 2:36)!

Give Me your heart, My son, My daughter!

The song that every servant of Jesus Christ carries in his heart is love for Jesus Christ, who suffered and died on the cross but who was raised as Lord of all. We must guard our hearts above all else. David Holdaway is a teacher of personal and national revival. He lives in South Wales and has written numerous books on the subject. One of my favorites is *The Captured Heart* (www.lifepublications.org. uk), in which he emphasizes that what captures our hearts will control our life and determine our destiny. He reminds us that when God is looking to raise someone up to use as His servant, He does not look at their social standing or academic qualifications, but at their heart. "Give Me your heart, My son! Give Me your heart, My daughter! Let your eyes delight in My ways!"

How often have we said, "I really want to love God and serve Him alone," and then stop and give up because we don't have the strength to serve Him without reservation. God understands that we are focusing on the wrong thing. He says to us, "Let My love for you, that I have given to you by the sacrifice of My Son, possess you in every area of your life. Receive My gift of freedom. Allow My Spirit to remold you into the image of My Son."

When we fully receive that gift, we no longer simply try to serve God or people in our own strength; we do not have to force ourselves to love others. Instead, we become captured by God's love and are transformed into loving persons and servants of the Lord. God does not just love; He *is* love. In the same way, love is not just something we do. Love becomes who we are.

We begin by giving God our hearts and confessing that our desire is to become like Jesus. When we do, our Risen Lord will give us the gift that will transform us into His servants and equip us to do His will. This gift is the "promise of His Father" that He is sending to us. Then we will be "clothed with power from on high" (Lk. 24:49).

Hymn for Contemplation and Worship

<u>Jesus is LORD!</u>
There is a **Name** above all names.
There is a **Light** unto all men.
There is a **Star** that early rises,
and a **Son** that never sets.
There is a **Rock** we must build on.
There is an **Anchor** for our souls.
There is a **Shepherd** of lost sheep
Who gave His **Life** to make us whole.

Chorus
There is a **Man**–Who knows what you're feeling.
There is a **Prince**–Who offers His Peace.
There is a **King**–Who came as a **Servant** to this world.
There's a **Life** and a **Love** that cannot cease.
There is a **NAME!**
Jesus is LORD!

He is the **Word** that became flesh.
He is the **Bread** that brings us Life.
He is the **Son** who shows us the **Father**
and the **One** who gives us sight.
Jesus is all that we must know.
Jesus is more than words can say.
Jesus is ever, only worthy
to receive undying praise.

Chorus
There is a **Man**–Who knows what you're feeling.
There is a **Prince**–Who offers His Peace.
There is a **King**–Who came as a **Servant** to this world.

There's a **Life** and a **Love** that cannot cease.
There is a **NAME!**
Jesus is LORD!

Please see the following references: Phil. 2:10-11; Acts 4:12; 3 Jn. 7; Rev. 2:3+ John 1:4-5; 2Pet. 1:19; Rev. 22:16; Jn. 1:15-18; Acts 4:10-12; Eph. 2;20-22; 1Pet. 2:4-8; Heb. 6:18-19; Jn. 10:1-18; Rom. 1:17; 1 Co. 1:30; 2Co. 5:14-21; Mt. 8:20; 9:6; 17:22; Isa. 53:5; Is. 9:6-7; Phil. 2:5-11; Jn. 1:14; Jn. 6:44-46; Jn. 6; 8:12-59

Chapter Four

The Servant's Power

I have put My Spirit upon him (Is. 42:1).

The First Suffering Servant Song (Is. 42:1-4)

"I have put My Spirit upon him." This was God's first promise to His servant (Is. 42:1). "The Spirit of the Lord is upon Me." These were Jesus' first words as He began His servant ministry (Is. 61:1; Lk. 4:18). When Jesus came into the world as God's Suffering Servant, He did not come alone. His Father was always with Him. His Spirit—for the Holy Spirit is the Spirit both of the Father and of Jesus—never left His side. Jesus' mother conceived and gave birth through the power of the Holy Spirit; so the Spirit lived in Jesus from the moment of conception. The Spirit taught Jesus the ways of God throughout His childhood and youth. Then when Jesus was about 30 years old and was baptized by John in the Jordan River, the Holy Spirit, who lived in Jesus, came upon Him in bodily form like a dove and empowered Him for His task. His Father spoke to Him from heaven and said, "You are My beloved Son; with You I am well pleased" (Lk. 3:21-22). The Gospel writer Luke emphasized the work of the Holy Spirit more than the other gospels. He later said, "And Jesus, full of the Holy Spirit ... was led by the Spirit" into the wilderness to be tempted by the devil, so that he could become the Great High Priest who could identify both with humans who suffer and are tempted and also with the Father, and become the intercessor for all who would come to the Father through Him. Then Jesus returned to Galilee in the power of the Holy Spirit to begin His ministry (Lk. 4:1,14). Truly, God "put His Spirit upon" Jesus.

Isaiah prophesied about this gift of the Spirit in his first Suffering Servant song. "Behold My Servant, whom I uphold: My chosen one in whom My soul delights! I have put My Spirit upon him; He will bring forth justice to the nations" (Is. 42:1 NASB). We who are followers of Jesus recognize that God the Father was speaking through the prophet Isaiah as He expressed His delight in His Son.

We also realize that God is speaking about all His people, because He was calling all Israel to become His servants to fulfill His promise to Abraham, so that all the families of the earth would be blessed through him (Gen. 12:1-3). But Israel refused to become servants of the world. So God Himself came as a servant. He continues to call all His followers to become His servants, so that we may become partners with Jesus to spread His blessing to the world. The Holy Spirit continues to remold the image of Christ within us, that we may become His servants to do the same works as God's Servant Jesus did. Servants are those who confess with Jesus that we have come into the world to do God's will.

God's First Gift to His Servants

It is fitting, then, that God's first gift to His servants is the Holy Spirit, for only by the Spirit can we do the works of the Lord (Is. 42:1). The four things that God did through His Spirit to establish Jesus in His ministry are exactly the four things He does for His servants today. First, the Spirit enabled Jesus to be born as a human; He also enables us to be born again into God's Kingdom (Jn. 3:5). Second, the Spirit filled Jesus with power for His mission; we also must be filled with the Spirit for the task ahead. Third, the Spirit strengthened Jesus through God's Word to overcome the temptations of the devil; the same

Spirit strengthens us, especially through God's Word, to overcome temptations from the devil. Fourth, the Spirit continued to lead and empower Jesus daily to complete the work the Father gave Him to do. Our life as servants is possible only as we allow the Spirit to lead us and strengthen us to complete the work God has given us to do. Just as Jesus' disciples were equipped to become servants at Pentecost, so we also must receive His power. Pentecost can never be repeated; but the miracle of the Pentecost experience must take place in the life of every servant of the Lord.

Have you ever been surprised, as a servant of the Lord, that you sometimes are able to do things that you could never have done in your own strength? Or how God uses you more effectively and powerfully at your weakest moment? Perhaps you have had times of deep insights into God's Word that you cannot explain by your human intelligence alone. You need not be surprised, for God promises His Holy Spirit to His servants. Remember His promise: "Behold My servant, whom I uphold, My chosen, in whom My soul delights; I have put My Spirit upon him" (Is. 42:1). He does not expect us to live the servant life with our own wisdom or power, for it is "not by might nor by power, but by My Spirit, says the Lord" (Zech. 4:6 NASB).

The Holy Spirit baptizes all Christians into the body of Christ.

Let's start at the very beginning. How does the Holy Spirit work in our lives? He begins by making His home inside every Christian. Paul expresses it clearly in Romans 8:9—"Anyone who does not have the Spirit of Christ does not belong to Him!" On the evening of the day He rose from the dead, Jesus appeared to His disciples and blessed them with His peace (John 20:19-23). Then He breathed into them His Holy Spirit, and Ezekiel's prophecy was finally fulfilled!

Hundreds of years before Christ entered the world as a human, God told Ezekiel to prophesy to the "breath"—that is, the Holy Spirit—to

28

breathe on the dry bones. Immediately "the breath came into them, and they lived and stood on their feet" (Ezek. 37:9-10 NJB)! God spoke to Ezekiel and told him that these bones were the whole house of Israel; they even spoke of themselves by saying "Our bones are dried up, and our hope is lost" (Ezek. 37:11). God was promising them that He would revive them, give them new life by freeing them from captivity, and would bring them back to their homeland. But we know that the Holy Spirit did not actually enter the people of Israel, for the Spirit was not given until Jesus was raised from the dead. Ezekiel prophesied, through this symbolic story of the dry bones, of the breath that would enter into His people at that time, but of the abundant life that would enter them at a much later time.

Ezekiel's prophecy was fulfilled when Jesus came into the world, ushering in the Kingdom of God. Jesus' first gift to His disciples on that Resurrection evening was the gift of the same indwelling Spirit who lived in Him (John 20:19-23). The Spirit of the Risen Lord entered into the disciples and applied Jesus' salvation to their lives! As it was with the disciples so it is with us. The Spirit comes into us at the moment we accept Jesus Christ as our Lord and Savior. His first action is to baptize us into the body of Christ (1 Cor. 12:13), for He knows that we cannot live the Christian life on our own. The Holy Spirit takes people who were non-kindred and transforms them into God's new supernatural family. The Holy Spirit creates the new family of God, whose members are closer sometimes to one another than to actual blood relatives.

The Indwelling Spirit

Who is this Spirit who indwells us? Isaiah tells us seven things about the indwelling Spirit, and how He works inside us to prepare us for servant ministry (Is. 11:1-2).

1. He is the Spirit of the Lord, the Spirit of Jesus and of the Father. The Spirit's greatest gift is intimacy with Jesus and the Father.

29

2. He is the Spirit of wisdom. He teaches us how to use knowledge. Every day we are overwhelmed with knowledge and new information. But do we know how to use that knowledge in a way that will give glory to God? We have a Teacher who fills us with wisdom to live in a way that glorifies God.
3. He is the Spirit of understanding, of insight and discernment.
4. He is the Spirit of counsel; He advises and guides us.
5. He is the Spirit of might; He strengthens our inner being with the spiritual qualities a servant needs and endues us with power to overcome evil.
6. He is the Spirit of knowledge, especially the knowledge of God, and knowledge of His Word. He teaches God's servants the Word of God, so that we may fill the world with the knowledge of God!
7. He is the Spirit of the fear of the Lord. He gives us strength to turn away from evil and sin, and to commit ourselves wholeheartedly to God and His will.

Paul adds, in Romans 5:5, that "God's love has been poured into our hearts through the Holy Spirit who has been given to us." The Greek word for love in this passage is *agape,* God's supernatural, unconditional, unlimited and transforming love. Here is the answer to how we can be known as Jesus' servants, or disciples, in the world: by obeying Jesus' command to love one another just as He has loved us (Jn. 13:34)! How can we obey this seemingly impossible command? By allowing the indwelling Holy Spirit to activate the supernatural *agape* love that He already has poured into our hearts. The same Spirit who raised Jesus Christ from the dead now dwells in you!

Jesus Christ baptizes His servants with the Holy Spirit.

You may have noticed that we have used the word "baptized" two times. This is not a mistake; the Holy Spirit baptizes us and Jesus also baptizes us with the Holy Spirit. All servants must have these two baptisms. The Holy Spirit baptism Paul mentions in 1 Corinthians 12:13 is done by the Spirit Himself, to place us inside the body of Christ. The Holy Spirit baptism that Luke speaks of in Acts chapter one is done by Jesus. The first baptism is one of position, or belonging; becoming members of God's Church. The second baptism is one of power, becoming equipped to proclaim the Gospel of the Kingdom to the world. Which one will you choose? The answer is you have no choice! The Spirit has already baptized you if you are a Christian; you must recognize that baptism and rejoice in the Spirit's gift of life in His supernatural community. Now you must allow Jesus to baptize you with the supernatural power of His Spirit, so that you may be His witnesses to the world.

All four Gospels prophecy that Jesus will baptize His followers with the Holy Spirit. Jesus Himself commanded His disciples not to leave Jerusalem until they were clothed with power from on high (Lk. 24:49). He then gave them His promise, in Acts 1:4-5 and 1:8. "You will be baptized with the Holy Spirit not many days from now ... you will receive power *(dunamis)* when the Holy Spirit has come upon you, and you will be My witnesses in all Judea and Samaria, and to the end of the earth."

But how easy it is to be misled, either by those who teach from a position that denies one or the other of the two baptisms, or by teachers who avoid the subject entirely. Such was the case with my family. We left our home country for our newly adopted country of Korea as a young couple full of excitement, expectation, and commitment to be God's witnesses in this new land. We had intellectual knowledge of the Holy Spirit but were lacking in experiential knowledge.

After some years, we were invited by our denomination to begin campus ministry at Seoul National University's college of Engineering, and were assigned to minister with Elder Kim Duk Young. She previously had been a missionary to Russia in her younger years; but her last ministry, which she began only after she was sixty years old, was to serve university students. Singlehandedly, this great woman of God established Christian Student Fellowships on six major university campuses in Seoul. We had the privilege of serving with her in her last ministry, on the national university campus; but only later did we learn why God placed us under this remarkable servant of the Lord, a precious treasure of the Korean Church. We watched her in her prayer life, and in her inspired ministry to the students, and wondered how she could be so effective in ministry. She had an "anointing" which we clearly lacked. One day she confided in me, and told me there was just one thing she hoped I would remember. "My ministry has been like the ministry of Elijah," she said, "breaking the strongholds of the devil on this great campus. Now I am waiting for Elisha to complete this ministry."

When Elijah completed his ministry and was ready to be taken up to heaven by a whirlwind, he told young Elisha to ask what he could do for him. Elisha knew the secret of his master's powerful ministry, so he replied, "please let there be a double portion of your Spirit on me" (2 Kin. 2:1-14).

Thus began our search for the power of the Holy Spirit. I now understand why God placed us in the leading university of Korea to begin our search. He had planted His Spirit-led servants in that great university, not only Elder Kim Duk Young but also Professor Hwang Hee Yoong, an outstanding scholar who ministered life to his students; and there were many others. I had seen the Holy Spirit move in power in an academic community; but I wanted to search the Scriptures to see what God has promised to all His servants. Beginning in Genesis, I carefully studied what the Bible teaches about the Holy Spirit. When I had read as far as Isaiah, I discovered that God promised the gift of His Spirit to His servants. Isaiah closes his teaching on the Suffering Servant with a song about the promise of the Holy Spirit. Jesus Himself read this song when He began His public ministry.

The Spirit of the Lord GOD is upon me,
because the LORD has anointed me
to bring good news to the poor;
he has sent me to bind up the brokenhearted,
to proclaim liberty to the captives,
and the opening of the prison to those who are bound;
to proclaim the year of the LORD's favor,
and the day of vengeance of our God;
to comfort all who mourn;
to grant to those who mourn in Zion,
to give them a beautiful headdress instead of ashes,
the oil of gladness instead of mourning,
the garment of praise instead of a faint spirit;
that they may be called oaks of righteousness,
the planting of the LORD,
that he may be glorified.
They shall build up the ancient ruins;
they shall raise up the former devastations;
they shall repair the ruined cities,
the devastations of many generations.
Is. 61:1-4 (see also Luke 4:16-21)

I was not aware of another important thing that was happening during those 10 years that we tried to work as missionaries without the empowering of the Holy Spirit. We discovered it only after we experienced this marvelous gift. We felt led to visit Jesus Abbey and tell Fr. Archer Torrey about our experience. It was then that he told us that since the first day we met in 1961 until we experienced the Holy Spirit in 1972, he had prayed every day, without missing even one day, for us to be baptized and filled with the Holy Spirit. "I came near to giving up on you after seven years," he said. "But God told me to pray until it happened." Are you aware that God has called people to pray for you, even people you may not know?

You are a servant of the Lord, called and empowered by the Lord Himself, that you may proclaim the Good News of God's Kingdom to the world, both with a life that is enriched and controlled by God's Spirit and with the dynamite-like power (*dunamis*) that God's Spirit gives you. The world will see your life of love, and recognize that you are Jesus' disciple. And the world will be transformed, not by your power, but by the Spirit's power that has come upon you.

Become a servant of the Lord who is led by the Spirit of God.

You will have a growing desire to glorify God through your life of holiness and your obedience to follow His Spirit's leading. You will be filled with new joy. God's Word will "come alive" in your life and guide you into all truth; and you will say to one another the words of the two disciples who met the Risen Lord on the road to Emmaus: "Did not our hearts burn within us while He talked to us ... and opened to us the Scriptures" (Luke 24:32)? Your loneliness will be transformed into solitude, as you enjoy God's presence. Those around you will notice that you are becoming more like the Lord who called you to be His servant. You will discover a new power to overcome sin and be free from bondages. You will become bolder for the Lord, but your boldness will be a "humble boldness." You will begin to be surprised at your own desire to go beyond yourself and give yourself to the world, for Christ's sake. You will become increasingly dissatisfied with living in your "comfort zone," as the Spirit enlarges the borders of your heart. And you will find a new love for your brothers and sisters in the *koinonia* fellowship of the Spirit. Most important, you will have a burning heart for the Lord that causes you to desire to complete the mission that God has prepared for you.

Hymn for Contemplation and Worship

<u>The Spirit of the Lord</u>

The Spirit of the Lord is on me, is on me.
I come to preach good news to the poor,
to call the captives free,
and cause the blind to see,
to speak the favored year of the Lord,
    of the Lord,
proclaim the favored year of the Lord.
(Is. 61:1-2; Lk. 4:18-19)

The Father has sent me;
I send you, I send you.
The works that I have done, you shall do.
Within your lives receive the Spirit as I breathe.
Go forth and bear much fruit. I send you, I send you.
The Father has sent me; I send you.
(Jn. 20:21-22; 14:12; 15:1-17)

And in the final days, says the Lord,
    says the Lord,
My Spirit on all flesh, I will pour:
on daughters and on sons,
on old men and the young
on men and women both, I will pour, I will pour.
My Spirit on all flesh, I will pour.
(Joel 2:28-29; Acts 2:17-18)

Full with the Spirit now,
we are one, we are one,
one Body called to labor and pray.
Who labors in the Lord

shall find a good reward,
and enter perfect joy on that Day, on that Day,
shall enter perfect joy on that Day.
(Jn. 16:12-15; 1 Cor. 12:13; Gal. 3:26-28; Eph. 4:1-16; Mt. 25:21; 2
Tim. 4:7-8)

I wrote this in honor of Dr. Alice Matthews, who retired from the
faculty of Gordon-Conwell Seminary in 2005. Alice has had a special
passion for effective ministry among and by women in the church,
and I tried to capture some of her heartbeat in, especially, verse 3 of
this hymn.

The Pentecost promise of the Spirit's outpouring upon all flesh—
male and female alike—reminded me of all the promises surrounding
the Spirit's ministry, and I have tried to show an unfolding in these four
verses, showing the biblical texts I was musing on as I wrote.

Before ascending to the Father in Acts 1:4-5, Jesus speaks to the
disciples; "Do not leave Jerusalem, but WAIT for the gift my Father
promised, which you have heard me speak about. For John baptized
with water, but in a few days you will be baptized with the Holy Spirit."
Jesus follows with the promise in Acts 1:8 that "you will receive power
(dunamis) when the Holy Spirit comes on you; and you will be my witnesses in Jerusalem, in all Judea, and Samaria, and to the ends of the
earth." We, therefore, dare not become servants of the Lord without
waiting upon the Holy Spirit's power.

As David Ross writes, "You are a servant of the Lord, called and
empowered by the Lord Himself, that you may proclaim the Good
News of God's Kingdom to the world, both with a life that is enriched
and controlled by God's Spirit and with the dynamite-like power
(dunamis) that God's Spirit gives you. The world will see your life
of love, and recognize that you are Jesus' disciple. And the world will
be transformed, not by your power, but by the Spirit's power that has
come upon you." Amen!!

The hymn is suitable, I believe, for the season of Pentecost. It celebrates both the outpouring of the Holy Spirit and the birth of the Church. The Spirit enables us—the Body of Christ—to walk in the good works God has prepared in advance for us (Eph. 2:10). The tune will be familiar to some as that used for the hymn, "What Wondrous Love is This?"

Chapter Five

The Servant of Justice

I will plant the seed of God's Word throughout Norway.
Hans Nielsen Hauge

I remember vividly when I was very young, my Sunday School teacher required me to study the catechism, which was a small book containing questions and answers to the basic doctrines of the Christian faith. We were required to memorize the answers to all the questions of the Westminster Shorter Catechism, which was prepared to instruct children in the content of the faith. The first question was "What is the chief end (or purpose) of man?" The answer was, "The chief end of man is to glorify God and enjoy Him forever."

Although I was unaware of the importance of the catechism at that time, that simple answer has remained in my mind to this day; it has reinforced my understanding of the message of the Bible. And I believe it was very influential in setting me on the path to becoming a servant of God and to knowing my chief purpose in life. Jesus the Servant glorified His Father by completing the work that God had given Him to do; and He did it with great joy (Jn. 17:4). I also, as a servant of the Lord, desire to glorify my Father by completing the work He has given me to do.

The Common Mission of All Servants

Each servant is unique and therefore receives a unique mission in life. But all servants have one purpose in common; we are called to do the same works Jesus did. Jesus Christ, the Suffering Servant of love, came into the world to establish God's justice among the nations. Isaiah speaks of Him this way: "I have put My Spirit upon Him; He will bring forth justice to the nations ... He will not grow faint or be discouraged till He has established justice in the earth" (Is. 42:1,4). "The Lord is exalted in justice, and the Holy God shows Himself holy in righteousness" (Is. 5:16).

We are called as servants to establish God's justice in the world. Some may disagree and argue that to love is the most important thing we can do in the world. But justice is not separate from love. God expresses His love in holiness and righteousness, so His justice is His act of love. What about mercy? God's justice is filled with His mercy. The apostle James reminds us that mercy triumphs over judgment. Mercy does not remove justice; it is God's power that enables justice to sustain, protect and give life to those in need (James 2:13). Then what about peace? Is it not what the world needs most? The psalmist replies, "Justice and peace kiss one another" (Ps. 85:10). Jesus performed many acts of love; He showed mercy to sinners and outcasts; He came as the Prince of peace, and one of His last words to His disciples was "Peace be with you." But He did all these things to reveal the righteousness and justice of His Father.

Where can justice be found?

But where can justice be found in this troubled world? The suffering world cries out for justice, and God demands it. "But let justice roll down like waters, and righteousness like an ever-flowing stream" (Amos 5:24). It can be found in the cross and resurrection of Jesus Christ. Justice begins with the redeeming work of Christ on

Calvary. Paul tells us that we have been justified by God's grace as a gift, through the redemption that is in Christ Jesus (Rom. 3:24). He then confirms this truth in Romans 5:1 – "Therefore, since we have been justified by faith, we have peace with God through our Lord Jesus Christ." But it does not end with justification by faith. When we are saved and declared righteous by God, our hearts immediately go out to the poor, and to those who suffer injustice and abuse.

Tim Keller once remarked that people who are into justification by faith as their main concern tend to be nervous around people who speak of justice; and people who are concerned only with ministering to the poor and needy tend to shy away from talking about justification by faith. So the issue that divides us and causes unbelievers to dismiss the church as irrelevant is our lack of understanding of God's justice. It is imperative that a servant of the Lord understands God's justice, because the servant's main task is to establish justice in the world.

The Biblical Meaning of Justice

We are justified by faith. We begin with God's act of justice on our behalf. Paul expressed it clearly in Romans 5:1-2 – "Therefore, since we have been justified by faith, we have peace with God through our Lord Jesus Christ. Through Him we have also obtained access by faith into this grace in which we stand, and we rejoice in hope of the glory of God."

What happened when we were saved? Isaiah 53 gives us the answer, and the Apostle Paul confirms it: Christ, who knew no sin, became sin on our behalf and freed us from bondage to Satan. What is more remarkable is that we have become the righteousness of God (2 Cor. 5:17-21)! We are not only forgiven, but we also have a new status: we become people who practice righteousness and justice in the world. We are freed from Satan's bondage. What do we do with our new freedom? Paul gives the answer: "You were called to freedom, brothers and sisters. Only do not use your freedom as an opportunity for the flesh, but through love serve one another" (Gal. 5:13).

We must proclaim the justice of salvation. God calls all of His servants to proclaim the Gospel of the Kingdom to the whole world. Matthew tells us that "this gospel of the kingdom will be proclaimed throughout the whole world as a testimony to all nations, and then the end will come (Matt. 24:14)." When Jesus appeared to His disciples after His resurrection, He told them that they would become His witnesses in Jerusalem and in all Judea and Samaria, and to the end of the earth (Acts 1:8).

We must practice justice in the world. The justice of God does not stop with our proclaiming God's salvation to the world. He has set us free to work for justice in the world. Isaiah 58 shows us how to begin, using fasting as an example. He tells us that God does not desire fasting as a mere formal act of worship; rather, God desires a fast that breaks the yoke of the oppressed and sets the captives free. It was God's Spirit who put the words into the Apostle James' mind when he said, "What good is it, my brothers and sisters, if someone says he has faith but does not have works? ... Faith by itself, if it does not have works, is dead ... I will show you my faith by my works" (James 2:14,17-18).

How do we know that we have been born again? We know it because we have confessed with our mouths that Jesus is Lord and believe in our hearts that God raised Him from the dead (Rom. 10:9). But we know it also because when we see those who are hungry, or who suffer racial discrimination, or who are victims of violence, our hearts immediately reach out to them in mercy, and we begin to seek ways to free them from human oppression.

In a world where over half of the world's net worth belongs to the top one percent of people; where there are more than 26 million refugees, half under the age of 18; where prejudice and discrimination against people of color is increasing; where millions of homeless children wander the streets of the world, many of whom are sexually abused; where the persecution of Christians as well as people of other religions has dramatically increased in the 21st century; where families are separated in their own nation, such as Korea, which has been divided over 75 years by foreign powers ... in such a world as this, God is calling His servants to rise up in love and become His servants of justice. All Christians are called to the ministry of reconciliation and justice in the world.

God plants His servants in every nation.

God plants His servants in every nation of the world, but very few of those servants change the destiny of a nation as did Hans Nielsen Hauge. He was an example of a Christian who blessed his own nation because of his new life in Christ. Born in the spring of 1771, when Norway was controlled by Denmark and its people suffered under religious darkness and industrial dormancy, God used him to awaken his people from their deep sleep of spiritual and economic bondage.

"The apostle of Norway!" This is how he is remembered today. But the church of his day did not recognize him as such. Most of the pastors of his day were ignorant of the Bible and did not preach the gospel of Jesus Christ; worse, they persuaded local officials to prohibit by law any lay person from preaching or publicly declaring the truth of the gospel. Hans was raised in a devout Christian home and valued the Bible. Some pastors encouraged him, but most criticized him. The result was that society in general viewed Hans and other young men like him—young men who loved God's Word, prayed and lived out their faith—as people who restricted their brains and who had become unbalanced in their minds, all because they read and acted out the Word of God.

He asked questions that Christians of his day refused to ask: What is the nature of our responsibility to the world? How do we practice righteousness and justice in such a way that we can change our nation and the world? Many Christians today would still have doubts about young Hans; for today's church remains largely uncommitted to the biblical teaching of righteousness and justice. While we argue over whether Christians should just proclaim good news of salvation by faith or whether we should also be involved in obliterating poverty and injustice in the world, the world continues to burn. The poor nations continue to receive inadequate health care. An example is the distribution of the covid-19 vaccine; millions of people have not received the vaccine early enough to protect them from the virus, because the rich nations have already bought up most of the vaccines, and pharmaceutical corporations will not share their intellectual property with the poor nations. Even when the poorer nations receive large quantities of the vaccine, corrupt governments often charge for the service that should be free, preventing the poorest of the poor from ever receiving help. The church remains silent.

But young Hans was not silent. He felt the call of God to preach the Gospel of Christ to his people. He did not feel called to become a pastor, but rather a layman who could persuade other lay people to live according to God's will. The key to his life was Matthew 6:33 (NASB) – "But seek first His kingdom and His righteousness, and all these things will be added to you."

This made everything he did illegal. God gave this young man understanding of how the Word of God can change a nation. He preached on this text more often than any other. He encouraged people to believe and be saved from sin, and then to act on the Word. "Work and pray" was his message to them. He maintained that if we would observe, follow and do what God's Word teaches, God would brighten homes and the community, and would bless their land.

Hans was a hard worker. He labored diligently on his father's farm and learned cabinet making. But his main interest was the salvation of his people of Norway. He knew that God's justice begins with deliverance from the bonds of Satan to new life in Jesus Christ. He experienced the power of the Holy Spirit, and the Spirit opened his eyes to new light in God's Word.

The Bible was the key to Hans' whole life and work.

The Word of God defined this young man and led him to the healing and empowering of his nation of Norway. He began to have a vision of what he could become as an instrument of the Lord, and of the unlimited potential of his nation. He once said, "I have the Lord's blessed unrest in my body, and anxiety in my soul to see that God's work is not neglected." He became a very popular Bible teacher who did not limit himself to spiritual interpretation but rather also pointed to the direction the nation could move if people based their lives on God's Word.

As A. M. Arntzen says in his excellent biography, "Hauge's pet idea was not only to broadcast the seed of God's Word throughout the land; but also to plant God's loyal citizens here and there throughout Norway, that they could show by example how to live a Christian life, and also build up strong, Christian communities". (The Apostle of Norway, A. M. Arntzen, Wipf and Stock Publishers, Eugene, Oregon; p. 221)

This was the secret of Hans' success: the Bible! He maintained that if a nation would base its constitution on the Bible, it could build a just and righteous society that provides for the needs of all its citizens, and would bless the entire world. He bore fruit that remained, trusting in the God's words through the prophet Hosea, "from Me comes your fruit" (Hos. 14:9).

By the time he had reached the age of 32, already there were several thousand young men and women preaching the Gospel throughout Norway. They formed communities based on the Word of God. Their slogan was "Work and Pray." God gave these young people an understanding of how His Word can change a nation. They began looking for possibilities for new industries. They took seeds whenever they went to a town or village to preach, so that farmers could plant them and produce new crops. They bought factories to produce their own goods without having to import them from Denmark and Holland. They learned that the laws of nature harmonize with God's spiritual laws! They learned to use the waste from fish in the villages near the water, to make fertilizer to grow crops. Hans continued to tell them that there is enough power in God's Word to change the whole world.

When Hans Nielsen Hauge looked out upon a harbor, he saw a future trading post, or a paper mill. He encouraged people with money to invest and urged them to make their nation self-sufficient without importing vital goods. When he discovered that there was a shortage of salt, he learned to process salt and to find good locations to produce salt, all the while preaching on the "salt of God's Word." He could have become a rich man, but the last time he was imprisoned—and he was imprisoned nine times for refusing to stop preaching and "interfering" with the establishment—he had only the equivalent of US$2.50 in all of his belongings. He had given all his money to farmers so they could buy land, or to entrepreneurs to start new businesses.

He taught the Bible. He planted human "trees" of God's Word throughout Norway, and they began to bear fruit and spread beyond the boundaries of Norway, to nations beyond.

Hans Nielsen Hauge's Legacy

Hans Nielsen Hauge's legacy of servant ministry is not forgotten. I first heard about this remarkable young man through my dear friend the late Frank Kaleb Jansen. Frank was gifted in many ways, like the young Hans Nielsen Hauge. Statesman, diplomat, missiologist, musician, member of the Nobel Peace Prize Committee, he was above all a servant of God's Word. He often said that he saw himself as "Joseph in Norway." He firmly believed that a nation that embraces the Bible as its foundation will prosper. In a conversation with a very important leader of North Korea, Frank spoke the same words that his mentor, Hans Nielsen Hauge had spoken. "If a nation will base its constitution on the Bible, it can build a just and righteous society that provides for the needs of all its citizens, and will bless the entire world." His words may not have been acceptable to the North Korean leadership, but they were definitely heard. Frank Kaleb Jansen was a servant, a very gentle and humble servant of the Lord. He modeled his life on Jesus Christ, the Suffering Servant, as the prophet Isaiah described Him: "A bruised reed He will not break, and a faintly burning wick He will not quench; He will faithfully bring forth justice. He will not grow faint or be discouraged till He has established justice in the earth; and the coastlands wait for His law" (Is. 42:3-4). Frank Kaleb was a friend of both North Korea and South Korea, and worked for peace on the peninsula. He also was God's servant of justice, including reconciliation for the broken nation of Korea. He made a significant impact on the mission of the Church throughout the world, through his book *Target Earth: The Necessity of Diversity in a Holistic Perspective.*

If you visit Jesus Abbey, a Christian community founded by R. A. Torrey III and deeply hidden in the hills of Kangwon Province, Korea, you will see this plaque on the wall: "Prayer Is Work; Work Is Prayer." Fr. Torrey also understood the truth that young Hans knew: If we believe the Word of God and act on it, God will use us to bring justice to our nation.

Many young men and women of Norway, and of nations around the world, continue to walk in the footsteps of Hans Nielsen Hauge. The psalmist's words give us hope: "Your people will volunteer freely in the day of Your power; in holy array, from the womb of the dawn, Your youth are to You as the dew" (Ps. 110:3 NASB). Servants of God's Word! Justice for the nations!

Hymn for Contemplation and Worship

Rule in This Place (Phil. 1:27; 2:1-5)

There is weakness in the church
when we fail to understand
that we're called to be God's *army* in the world.
But the battles that we wage
are too often with ourselves.
Lord, unite us 'neath the banner of Your love.

Grant us unity and openness,
humility and brokenness.
O Lord, release Your power in this place.
In Your brightness illumine us.
In Your righteousness, unbind us.
O Lord, release Your power in this place.

//: Rule in this place (4x)

There's a spirit in the world
that does not honor God.
And it holds the helpless masses in its power.
Oppressed by that dark foe,
they cannot see Your light.
O we pray for their salvation in this hour.

Bring the captives to Your Liberty,
the downcast to Your victory.
O Lord, release Your power in this place.
In Your brightness illumine us.
In Your righteousness, unbind us.
O Lord, release Your power in this place.

//: Rule in this place (4x) *

With the instability of politics fanned by the pandemic in recent days, the church of our Lord has not shown unity of the Spirit in the bond of peace, but rather has become very divisive and hostile to those who look, act and think differently than we do. This has been the weakness in the church throughout the history but more evident in these days in America. We need to realize 'the schemes of the enemy' that divide and blur our call to be "God's Army in this world."

This song is my prayer to our God to rule in His church and bring us back to His heart and will so that we can be what we are called to be in the world:

"Bring the captives to Your liberty,
the downcast to Your victory.
O Lord, release Your power in this place.
In Your brightness illumine us.
In Your righteousness, unbind us.
O Lord, release Your power in this place.
//: Rule in this place (4x)"

"Learn to do good; **seek justice**, correct oppression; bring justice to the fatherless, and plead the widow's cause" (Isa. 1:17).

"He has told you, O man, what is good; and what does the Lord require of you but to do justice, and to love kindness, and to walk humbly with your God?" (Mic. 6:8).

"Though we live in the world, we do not wage war as the world does. The weapons we fight with are not the weapons of the world. On the contrary, they have divine power to demolish strongholds. We demolish arguments and every pretension that sets itself up against

48

the knowledge of God, and we take captive every thought to make it obedient to Christ" (2 Cor. 10:3-5).

"But you are a chosen people, a royal priesthood, a holy nation, God's special possession, that you may declare the praises of him who called you out of darkness into his wonderful light" (1 Pet. 2:9).

"You were called to freedom, brothers and sisters. Only do not use your freedom as an opportunity for the flesh, but through love serve one another" (Gal. 5:13)!

"Jesus Christ, the Suffering Servant of love, came into the world to establish God's justice among the nations. Isaiah speaks of Him this way: "I have put My Spirit upon Him; He will bring forth justice to the nations ... He will not grow faint or be discouraged till He has established justice in the earth" (Is. 42:1,4). "The Lord is exalted in justice, and the Holy God shows Himself holy in righteousness" (Is. 5:16).

Chapter Six

The Servant of the Word

You have made Your Word great across all your heavens.
(Ps. 138:2 Robert Alter translation)

God's Word is the home of the servant. It is the secret place of the Most High, the servant's hiding place. There we meet our Father face to face each morning and behold the beauty of Jesus, the Father's final word to the world. In that meeting the Spirit opens the eyes and ears of our hearts to hear all that God has to say to us. The third Suffering Servant Song (Is. 50:4-9) is perhaps the most intimate of the four songs; there we discover that the servant sings for joy because God, his loving Father, awakens him morning by morning, so that His servant may hear Him speak words that will equip him to sustain the weary people of the world. The servant listens attentively as a disciple, as one whose greatest joy is to hear his Master speak.

John the Baptist was among the earliest of Jesus' servants, and he spoke of himself as the "friend of the bridegroom, who stands and hears him and rejoices at the bridegroom's voice." When He heard Jesus speak, he cried out, "This joy of mine is now complete" (Jn. 3:29)!

We all experience God in a variety of ways. The beauty of the graceful appearance of the morning light at dawn, or the splendors of a sunset, or simply walking with Jesus, enjoying His presence in the cool of the evening as we talk with Him and listen to Him; all these things deepen our communion with the Lord. But none of these ways can compare with hearing God speak in His Word.

Let the Word of God dwell in you richly.

Jesus Himself is the Word (John 1:1; 1 John 1:1). It is fitting, there-fore, that He chooses to speak to us in His Word. Life-changing com-munion with Christ must take place in His Word. My own experience as a servant of the Lord is Word experience. Here the truth about God, about the world, about life, and even about myself is made known to me.

When we allow God's Spirit to fill us with the Word of God, a miracle happens. God's Word makes its home in us. The Word brings us into the presence of God. His Word fills our minds with God's truth and our hearts with His love. Then God's Word will renew our thoughts, redirect our wills, restore our emotions, refocus our imagina-tion, rebuke our sin, rejoice our hearts, re-energize our bodies, restore our broken spirits, and redeem our lives. Is it any wonder, then, that the apostle Paul exhorts us to "let the word of Christ dwell in you richly, teaching and admonishing one another in all wisdom, singing psalms and hymns and spiritual songs, with thankfulness in your hearts to God" (Col. 3:16).

When a person understands even a little of God's Word, she knows that this is not just a human book. It is God's book that He opens to His servants each day. When God called Joshua to become the successor of Moses, He promised him that he would be able to lead the rebellious people of Israel out of the desert and into the Promised Land. Then He gave Joshua one major command: "This Book of the Law [the whole Word of God] shall not depart from your mouth, but you shall meditate on it day and night, so that you may be careful to do according to all that is written in it. For then you will make your way prosperous, and then you will have success" (Josh. 1:8).

The Centrality of God's Word

Perhaps you noticed as we talked about Hans Nielsen Hauge, a servant of justice for his nation of Norway, that he was never without his Bible. The Holy Spirit opened his eyes to new light in God's Word. God spoke to him of His mysteries about how his nation could overcome poverty and regain dignity. Just as He did for Joshua, so He did also for young Hans. He spoke to him each morning; He told him His will for each day; He gave His servant his "blueprint" for each day, instructing him in the way he should go. Hans understood Isaiah's description of the Word of God in the second Suffering Servant Song. "He made my mouth like a sharp sword ... He made me a polished arrow" (Is. 49:2). A sharp sword that pierces our hearts and reveals our sins but also God's will; a polished arrow that travels throughout our own nation and the world, to fill the world with the knowledge of God!

Jesus said that the words He spoke were Spirit and life (Jn 6:63). Millions of people have casually picked up a small pamphlet of the Gospel of John, and by reading it have received new, eternal life. The Holy Spirit is the author of God's Word, and He imparts life to those who seek God in His Word. God desires to meet His servants in His Word and to reveal to them His mystery, "which is Christ, in whom are hidden all the treasures of wisdom and knowledge" (Col. 2:2-3).

As a servant, do you not have questions that you would like to ask God? Do you not seek direction for the way you should live as a servant? The answer to every question in the world is hidden in our Father; and He chooses to give them to us in His Word.

As servants, we are called to become people of the Word, who know God and His will for our lives and for the world. Jesus said, "Man shall not live by bread alone, but by every word that comes from the mouth of God" (Matt. 4:4). As He prayed for His disciples, He said to His Father, "I have given them the words that You gave Me, and they have come to know the truth ... sanctify them in the truth; Your Word is truth" (Jn 17:8,17).

The *Psalms* are the key to understanding the whole Bible. They contain all the theology of the Bible, and they speak to every human emotion. Jesus prayed the psalms and very likely sang them with His disciples. We meet Jesus when we contemplate and pray the Psalms. Thomas Merton reveals their importance by saying, "*The Psalms* bring our hearts and minds into the presence of the living God. They fill our minds with His truth in order to unite us with His love" (*Bread in the Wilderness,* p. 13).

Listening to God in His Word

The third Suffering Servant Song of Isaiah (Is. 50:4-9) teaches us how God equips His servants with His Word. God speaks through His Word; the Bible is a vertical book. All other books are horizontal, man speaking to man. God's Word is permanent, eternal. "The grass withers, the flower fades, but the word of our God will stand forever" (Is. 40:8). His Word is truth, and Jesus says, "you will know the truth, and the truth will set you free" (John 8:32). Only the truth will set people free from their bondages, and God's servants must be filled with truth.

Isaiah wrote all four Suffering Servant songs to the Babylonian captives who had been freed by Cyrus (another servant of the Lord – see Isaiah 44:28-45:7). They still saw themselves as victims, and they even accused God of "divorcing their mother" and selling them into slavery (Is. 50:1-3)! Like so many suffering people today, they felt that God had abandoned them. Of course God has never abandoned His people in past times or today; He sends His servants of truth to set people free.

The entire third song is all about the truth of God, found only in His Word. We began by saying that God loves His servants so much that He wakes us up each morning. He "awakens my ear" to listen to what He has to say to me each day (Is. 50:4). These days many Christians have trouble hearing God. They seek new methods to be able to hear His voice; they often complain that today's world is so filled with noise and distractions that it is almost impossible for an active person to hear God speak. Do they need to go to a monastery? Or move to a quiet, idyllic village where they can hear Him? When our family lived in New York City, my office was located just two blocks from Times Square, one of the noisiest places in the world. One day I was walking in Times Square, surrounded by unceasing loud noise and glaring lights; I paused and asked God, "Can I actually hear you speak, Lord, in such a place as this? Please teach me how to hear You speak." God replied with these simple words: "Come closer, My son."

The answer is not found in methodology, or more study, or a change of physical location. It is found in a change of heart, by choosing to abide; that is, by resting, making our home in God through His Word. "If you abide in Me, and My words abide in you, ask whatever you wish, and it will be done for you" (Jn 15:7).

Two Words That Define a Servant's Heart

Two words define the heart of a servant: *listen* and *obey* (Is. 50:4-5). A servant listens as a disciple, so that he may know God's will and obey completely. In your reading through the Gospel accounts, have you not noticed how Jesus the Suffering Servant sought His Father each morning, and often throughout the night? Communion with His Father was the secret of Jesus' ministry; and their communion was centered on the words they shared. Jesus listened to each word His Father spoke to Him, and later shared them with His disciples. He listened and obeyed every word with unspeakable joy. This was His heart – the heart of the greatest Servant of all! Listen and obey; there is no other way.

His Father's words empowered Jesus to never turn backward but to set His face like flint, the hardest of stones, as He endured sufferings and the cross by obeying with joy (Is. 50:7)! There is no word of Scripture about which we can say "this has nothing to do with me," for each word is God speaking to me! I only need to listen and obey.

God's Word creates a new beginning.

Why is it that a servant must meet God and listen to Him in His Word? Because all ministry flows out of God's Word! Jesus said, "If you abide in Me, and My words abide in you, ask whatever you wish, and it will be done for you" (John 15:7). God makes new beginnings through His servants' obedience. His Word always creates a new beginning! God compared His Word to the rain and snow that come down from heaven. The rain and snow do not return there until they water the earth and enable it to provide food for His people. "So shall My word be that goes out from My mouth; it shall not return to Me empty, but it shall accomplish that which I purpose, and shall succeed in the thing for which I sent it" (Is. 55:10-11). Jesus Christ was the Word that God sent from heaven. Jesus the Word came to earth, and He did not return to the Father until He had accomplished God's purpose for sending Him. Listen to how He prayed His priestly prayer to the Father: "I glorified you on earth, having accomplished the work that You gave me to do" (Jn 17:4). He created a new beginning for all who would trust in Him. The same is true of God's words that He sends to His servants. They will create a new beginning; they will not return to God empty.

How can we become filled with the Word of God?

How then can the Word of God become the servant's weapon for spiritual warfare? The second Suffering Song describes the Word of God as being a "sharp sword and a polished arrow," both weapons for defeating Satan, the enemy (Is. 49:2).

How can we come to know God through His Word? How can we be so full of God's Word that we can walk in deep fellowship with Him each day?

Humility is the key. "But to this one I will look, to him who is humble and contrite of spirit, and who trembles at My Word" (Is. 66:2). Jesus shows us the way. He emptied Himself of all divine power and "made Himself nothing" (Phil. 2:7)! When we become nothing, God becomes everything in our life. He then fills us with His Word and with Himself. Those who tremble at God's Word understand that God's Word is absolute truth that will completely transform their lives. When we tremble at God's Word we become aware of our sinfulness and begin to repent. But as we continue listening to God speaking to us, we become filled with awe and wonder at the majesty of His Word that will replace our sorrows with His overwhelming joy. God tells us that He gives us His Word as our most powerful weapon to defeat the Enemy and to bring Kingdom life to the world.

We must make the Bible the chief book in our lives. There is a cost of close involvement with God and His Word. The great men and women of the Bible all knew this cost, the suffering and the risk of responding to God's word to them. But as they yielded to God's words, "they found themselves borne along, strangely free, confident, and even joyful, and were sustained to the very end of their lives by the majestic power and love that had at first so overwhelmed them" (Ronald S. Wallace, class notes at Columbia Theological Seminary, 1971).

We must remember what it will cost us to become able to understand, receive and live with the Word of God. It will demand hard work, denying ourselves many other pleasures, and prayer. As I sat under this extraordinary teacher of God, Ronald S. Wallace, I remember him telling us time after time that if we allow God's Word to dominate and mold our thinking as no other book can do, and if we take the trouble to read it daily so that we almost know it by memory, then the Bible will give itself to us "in an extraordinary way." As we keep seeking, we find; as we continue to knock, the door is open to us.

"We must allow God's Word to shape our minds. We have to let the Word dictate the way our thoughts have to go, the paths they have to follow, as we respond mentally. We have to yield up our self-will in the movement of our own minds, as we submit ourselves to the truth before us, and to God who Himself is before us in this truth. True knowledge of God is born out of obedience" (Ronald S. Wallace, The Lord Is King: The Message of Daniel. InterVarsity Press, Leicester, England, 1979. p.178).

How can we make God's Word central in our lives? Consider the following six ways we can allow God's Holy Spirit to reveal God's Word to us.

Read the Word of God. This is the best method of Bible study. The prophet Jeremiah lamented his people's ignorance of God's Word, that caused them to turn away from God. He cried out, "O land, land, land, hear the word of the Lord" (Jer. 22:29). If he were still with us, he would cry out loudly again today.

There are many ways to read God's Word, but the one thing they all have in common is that reading God's Word will enable us to hear God speak His words to us today. If we read the Word aloud, with one or more persons, we can hear the words, and we are doubly blessed. But even if we read alone, silently, we hear God speaking.

A good goal would be to read through the Bible at least once a year. If you fail to do it, don't allow yourself to be weighed down by guilt; just begin reading again. Remember, when we read the Bible we are partaking of our spiritual food. When we understand the whole message of the Bible, we have a wholesome and balanced diet that will nourish us spiritually. What method should we use? There are many methods, but I would recommend the reading method of Robert Murray M'Cheyne, a young Scottish servant of the Word who lived over a century and a half ago. If you follow his plan, which is available on the internet, you will be able to read through the Old Testament once and the New Testament and Psalms twice in a year. Another effective method, which I have used throughout my ministry, is to read through the Bible book by book, beginning in Genesis and ending in The Revelation to John; then begin again in Genesis and continue to read daily. I read from the Psalms each day. The method is not important; reading faithfully and regularly will bring change.

The most important thing to remember when reading the Bible is that we must expect God to speak to us as we read. God loves to meet us in His Word, and He desires to speak to us each time we read with a listening ear.

Study the Word of God. The more a servant reads God's Word, the greater the desire grows to study the Word. Once again, remember that all good Bible study begins by reading the Bible. If your local church or fellowship has a Bible study program, do not hesitate to become a part of a group Bible study. Study Bibles may help, but there is the danger that one may become too dependent on just one person, or a select group of people, to get understanding. The best tool for personal Bible study is a cross-reference Bible; you can find references in the margin for other Scriptures that speak of what you are reading. Remember: Scripture interprets Scripture. You may be surprised as you read the Psalms, for instance, that you gain much understanding from the references to passages in the Gospels or other parts of Scripture.

Two books that will help you are *How to Read the Bible for All Its Worth,* and *How to Read the Bible Book by Book,* both by Douglas K. Stuart and Gordon D. Fee. You can consult with your spiritual leaders to find good commentaries and other helps for study.

Meditate on the Word of God. Meditation on God's Word is the key to hearing God speak to us. The Word of God is alive, and this is where Jesus the Word meets us and speaks to us. This is where we meet God, and hear Him speak so we can have a "conversation with God." Dietrich Bonhoeffer, who was executed by the Nazi government because he opposed Hitler's demonic power, was a great meditator. When all of his students were forced to join Hitler's army, Bonhoeffer wrote to each of them every week, and shared with them the words of Scripture that he had meditated on and that strengthened him. Once someone asked him what he meant by meditation. He replied, "Accept the Word of scripture and ponder it in your hearts as Mary did. This is all. This is meditation ... We must put ourselves in the presence of God by slowly, quietly, patiently advancing from word to word, and pause over each verse to listen and wait for the Spirit to guide us" (Bonhoeffer, *Meditating on the Word,* pp. 51-52).

What happens when we meditate? We pause before each word and listen. God speaks. Then a miracle happens! The Holy Spirit plants each word in our inner being, so that the Word can create a new beginning. This is how it works: The Spirit plants the seed of God's Word in me as I listen to what God wants to say to me. I become the "planting of the Lord, that He may be glorified" (Is. 61:3); then the Holy Spirit "plants" me in the perfect position to bear fruit. When we bear fruit for the Lord, He is glorified. His Word does not return to Him empty.

A miracle took place some years ago at two major universities on America's East Coast: Brown University, and the Rhode Island School of Design (RISD), both located in Providence, Rhode Island. Ellen and I were ministering to students at Rutgers, the state university of New Jersey. Their student Christian fellowship was alive in God's Holy Spirit and in the Word of God. We taught them to meditate on the Bible, word by word, and to expect God to do something new. God led the students at Rutgers University to meditate corporately on the passage we mentioned earlier, the two verses from Isaiah that speak of new beginnings. "So shall My word be that goes out from My mouth; it shall not return to Me empty, but it shall accomplish that which I purpose, and shall succeed in the thing for which I sent it" (Is. 55:10-11). They did not understand the reason, but God's Spirit encouraged them to meditate on this one simple word for three weeks. As they meditated daily, their hearts began to burn within them.

During this time, friends who were studying at the Rhode Island School of Design (RISD) and Brown University contacted them and told them how envious they were; they had no church that could minister to them on their campuses, which were adjacent to one another. These students also were hungry for the Word of God. God then spoke to the students at Rutgers and explained to them that the reason He had them meditate so long on those two verses from Isaiah was that He wanted to start a "new beginning" among the students at RISD and Brown. The Rutgers students had nothing to offer except the word on which they had meditated and the mission God had given them. The result is that about twenty Christian "fools for Christ" drove in their old vans to these two schools and ministered the Word of God to their friends. What happened? A new beginning! God spoke; they listened; and God's Spirit made a new thing happen! Within a year, a new church was founded adjacent to the campuses of RISD and Brown University, with a young pastor who taught the Word of God! New life began to take place on these campuses! When servants hear God speak in His Word, new beginnings take place.

Pray the Word of God. Meditation is the bridge that connects godly Bible study with prayer. We study to learn about God and His will for our lives. Meditation makes the words of the Bible alive and personal, and they lead us into prayer.

Praying prayers of petition and thanksgiving, or of intercession for others should be part of our life with the Word of God. No prayers are greater, or more powerful, than those that use the actual words of the Psalms to pray. We are using God's own words, praying them just as we meditate on them in the Psalms; God's words then return to Him in prayer, having accomplished the purpose for which He sent them (Is. 55:10-11).

Memorize the Word of God. The beauty of memorization is that God's Word remains in your mind and heart, and He can speak to you continually through the "implanted Word" (James 1:21-22). Before you dismiss this discipline as being too difficult, consider two ways to memorize Scripture.

I have discovered that I am often effortlessly memorizing Scripture as I meditate on it, and the words remain with me. The Navigators' ministry has enabled many people to memorize Scriptures and store

THE SERVANT OF THE WORD

them in their minds. Matthew the Poor (Father Matta El-Meskeen , 1919-2006), one of the greatest Coptic Orthodox monks, gives us clear understanding of how to memorize the Bible. He speaks of "intellectual," or academic, memorization, which seeks to master the Bible so that we become able to use what we memorize to teach others (or perhaps to impress others). Over against this type of meditation, which makes the words of Scripture submit to us, he recommends "spiritual memorization," which requires us to be totally submitted to God's Word. Spiritual memorization could also be called "spiritual remembering" the words of Scripture. God gives us this gift when we understand His words, so that we may become witnesses for him. "The Helper, the Holy Spirit, whom the Father will send in My name, He will teach you all things and *bring to your remembrance* all that I have said to you" (Jn. 14:26). Bible memorization is a spiritual work that God gives to those who have been granted to be witnesses for Him. "When the Holy Spirit recalls certain words to us, He does so in depth and breadth, not simply reminding us of the text of a verse, but giving it with irresistible wisdom and spiritual power to bring out the glory of the verse and the power of God in it" (Matthew the Poor, The Communion of Love, St. Vladimir's Seminary Press, 1984, p. 18-20).

I actually learned "spiritual remembrance" from my father in-law, Dr. T. Layton Fraser, a pastor and former professor of Bible. He memorized the entire Book of Psalms by allowing the Holy Spirit to lead him into its spiritual depths. He preached often on a psalm, and he always began by simply speaking the words of the psalm. Then his congregation fixed their minds on the spiritual truth he fed them.

Youth With A Mission's *Word By Heart* program employs this concept of spiritual remembering in order to help a person become full of God's Word. Not by rote memorization, but by entering into a story, or event, or truth in Scripture and allowing the Spirit to give us spiritual insights into the Word of God. The result is that we can more easily remember it as we share with others the secrets of the Kingdom of God. Memorization becomes a form of meditation, fixing our eyes on each word, and rejoicing in it. The psalmist then enables us to confess the words of the psalmist: "I will delight in Your statutes; I will not forget Your Word" (Ps. 119:15)!

Proclaim the Word of God. God's Word completes its work in us when we proclaim it to others, through our words, but also through our lives. As we proclaim the truth of God's Word, we are continually renewed. People are healed, saved and made new through the power of the Word. And we have seen through the ministry of God's servant Hans Nielsen Hauge that nations can be completely transformed through God's Word.

Hymn for Contemplation and Worship

<u>To Hear as Those Well Taught</u>
(Is. 50:4-5; Ezra 7:10; 1 Tim. 4:16*)

The Sovereign LORD has given me
a well instructed tongue
that I might understand the word
that helps the weary one.
Each morning he awakens me
unto the word of God.
My ear he wakens, day by day,
to hear as those well taught.

The Sovereign LORD, has given me
an open, list'ning ear.
And I did not defy his will,
nor dare refuse to hear.
Each morning he awakens me
unto the word of God.
My ear he wakens, day by day,
to hear as those well taught.

God help us, who would dare to teach,
be swift ourselves to learn.
May Your word, like an untamed fire,
within our spirits burn.
Each morning, Lord, awaken us
unto the word of God.
Our ears awaken, day by day,
to hear as those well taught.

O, may I sing the Servant's song

in humble, holy fear.
Lord, grant to me a well-trained tongue
and open wide my ear.
Each morning, Lord, awaken me
unto the word of God.
My ear awaken, day by day,
to hear as those well taught.

The text was written in honor of Gordon Conwell's graduating class of 2005. I am continually challenged by this great "Servant Song" from Isaiah 50:4-5 and wanted to leave it as a challenge for the graduates. Of all the texts that I have shared with students through the years, this one probably tops the list of "most cited." It is part of one of the famed "Servant Songs" from Isaiah.

"The Sovereign LORD has given me a well-instructed tongue, to know the word that sustains the weary. He wakens me morning by morning, wakens my ear to listen like one being instructed. The Sovereign LORD has opened my ears; I have not been rebellious, I have not turned away" (Is. 50:4-5 NIV).

Christians have often seen these texts as ultimately embodied in our Lord Jesus. This passage reminds me of Jesus, in passages like Mark 1:35-39, rising up early to pray in lonely places and thus to discern the Father's direction for the day. This, apparently, He did often (Luke 5:16).

The text from Isaiah has some evocative language, especially in the Hebrew original. "The Sovereign LORD has given me the tongue of disciples," we are told. Some have actually thought that the Hebrew text needed correction at this point and thus changed it to read, "the tongue of a teacher" (so the NRSV). But it is our thinking, not the text, that needs correction. The NRSV notes say, "Is. 50:4 Cn: Heb. of those who are taught". Their notes reveal that the actual Hebrew is telling quite a different story than their own translation.

Our tongues—those untamable infernos in the middle of our faces (James 3:6)—must be well discipled if we would ever use them for good. How can this be done? Our ears must be ever opened to the Lord. Verse 5 reads, literally, "the Sovereign LORD dug ears in me, and I have not been rebellious." I pray this for myself—to be obedient to the fact that God gave me ears and, by using them well to listen to and be immersed in God's Word, to find my tongue becoming more and more tamed and useful for the Master.

Chapter Seven

The Servant of Love

I am madly in love with Jesus – Mother Teresa

For in this world, when we love as He loves, we are just like Him.
(1 Jn 4:17 First Nations Version)

January 8, 1956 was the day five young missionaries were martyred as they attempted to evangelize the Auca people of Ecuador. They were servants of love who had accepted the "dangerous privilege" of walking with their Lord wherever He would lead them. They fully understood the words of the apostle John: "By this we know love, that He laid down His life for us, and we ought to lay down our lives for the brothers" (1 Jn 3:16). Seven years before, Jim Elliot, one of the five, had written words in his journal that echoed the apostle John's words: "He is no fool who gives what he cannot keep, to gain that which he cannot lose."

The story did not end there. Jim's wife, Elisabeth, together with Rachel Saint, the sister of one of the martyred missionaries, returned to live and witness among the Auca peoples. This resulted in the conversion of the entire tribe to Jesus. Perhaps Elisabeth's most famous words were, "You are loved with an everlasting love." Her philosophy of life can be summed up by words she later wrote: "His grace is sufficient. We have proved beyond any doubt that God means what He says—nothing can separate us from the love of Christ. We pray that if any, anywhere, are fearing that the cost of discipleship is too great, they may be given a glimpse of that treasure in heaven promised to all who forsake."

"For from Him and through Him and to Him are all things."

This wonderful story of the lives of true servants of the Lord reveals a basic principle of how God works in the world. The apostle Paul tells us the principle. "For from Him and through Him and to Him are all things. To Him be glory forever. Amen" (Rom. 11:36). This was such a profound secret that Paul had to say "Amen" when he revealed it! He had to respond by worshiping God. We are reminded of the words that the eminent New Testament scholar Gordon D. Fee spoke in a lecture at Regent College, Vancouver: "True theology (study of God) must lead to doxology (praise to God)!" Paul's very next words were an appeal to all of God's servants to present their bodies as a living sacrifice, holy and acceptable to God, as an act of spiritual worship (Rom. 12:1).

Love flows from God. Jesus completed God's gift of love on the cross of Calvary, bringing salvation to the world. Only then did He return to His Father. We learned this truth when we spoke of God's Word not returning to Him void (Is. 55:10-11). Jesus came as the Word of God; and He did not return to God without accomplishing the purpose for which God sent Him. This same principle applies to all servants of God. We receive the fullness of God's love, grace upon grace; then His love flows through us to the world as we obey His will. The fruit of God's love then returns to our Father in heaven through the praises of those who have received God's love through our lives of service. As servants of God we also have an "inheritance that is imperishable, undefiled, and unfading, kept in heaven" for us (1 Pet. 1:4).

The principle remains the same. The depths of the riches and wisdom and knowledge of God reveal to us that "from Him and through Him and to Him are all things." It was true of Stephen, the first Christian martyr. As he was being stoned to death, Stephen gave to his enemies the love which he himself had received from God, by forgiving them. But did Stephen's act of love actually change the world? Yes, it did. Shortly after his death, the greatest enemy of the Church, who had been present at the stoning of Stephen, met Jesus Christ on the road to Damascus and became a follower of Jesus Christ. God used the apostle Paul as one of His servants to spiritually conquer the whole Roman Empire! God's love returned to Him through the conversion of innumerable people throughout the Roman Empire. All things that flow from God are love, because God is love. His Holy Spirit enables God's servants to spread that love to others; and love returns to God.

We must say yes to God.

God so loved the world that He sacrificed Himself to redeem it! Power, money, influence, war; none of these things change the world. Only the love of God can change the world. Servants enter the world with the weapon of love, which is more powerful than all powers of the world.

God loves without condition, and we are commanded to also love without conditions. As Hans Uhrs von Balthasar says in his excellent book *Love Alone is Credible* (Ignatius Press, 2004. p. 125): "Love is an a priori Yes to whatever may come, whether it be the Cross, or being plunged into absolute abandonment, or being forgotten, or utter uselessness and meaninglessness." It is the Son's Yes to the Father, young Mary's Yes to the angel when he told her that she would supernaturally become the mother of the Messiah. It is our absolute response to God's absolute love. Jesus the Servant changed the world. And He promises that those who follow Him and love as He loves will also change the world.

Another Young Woman Who Said Yes

Can we find such servants of love today? Let's ask a person who actually changed the nation of India—Mother Teresa of Calcutta, India—what she thinks about the servant life. In 1962 the Indian government awarded Mother Teresa the Padma Shri, one of its highest civilian honors, for her service to the people of India. She also received the Nobel Peace Prize in 1979.

As a young girl, only 18 years old, she said yes to God's love. When she left her home in Albania to eventually serve in Calcutta, India, her mother's parting words were, "Put your hand in Jesus' hand, and never let go." In her early years of ministry, her community leaders sometimes thought she was overly spiritual, almost mystical, because of her great love for Jesus and deep intimacy with God. But in her later years, as she ministered to the "poorest of the poor" in the dark slums of Calcutta, she could not find those same feelings of intimacy with Jesus. Nevertheless Mother Teresa never let go of Jesus' hand, even in the darkest nights of suffering in Calcutta. For some time she could no longer feel Christ's intimacy; but she continued to trust Him. She once spoke these words to Jesus: "Jesus, even though I cannot feel Your wonderful presence as I once did, I will always love you."

As I was reading some of her private writings that were made public after her death, I discovered some secrets of her life as a servant of the Lord that brought change not only to the nation of India but also to the world. Here are some of them.

Her great secret was her love for God. Her life and all that she did was based on the love that came to her from God, the love that worked through her for the suffering people of India, and the love that returned to God through her sacrificial life in her chosen nation.

She once remarked: "I am madly in love with Jesus!" She strongly maintained that "if one is not in love with God, one can never be a servant." She saw herself as a "carrier of God's love." In her own words,

"I have used every power in me to love Jesus blindly, totally, only." We must let God love us to the degree that His divine love permeates every fiber of our being. Jesus warned Peter that His love for him would radically change him and lead him eventually where he would not choose to go (Jn 21:18-19). When the little teenage girl Mary allowed God to love her, she became the mother of the Messiah. When Simon allowed God to love him, he became Peter. When Saul, the persecutor of the Church, allowed Jesus to love him, he became Paul. Young Agnes Gonxha Bojaxhiu became Mother Teresa.

She understood that to love is to obey. She was an obedient servant to the end of her life. She was faithful in pursuing God's call as a teenager; then throughout her life she obeyed God's call unconditionally. Jesus Himself said, "If you love Me, you will keep My commandments" (Jn 14:15). Mother Teresa vowed never to refuse God anything He asked of her.

She insisted that a servant must serve in community, never alone. When she first pursued her call to work among the poorest of the poor, she submitted her request to do so to her community. She then waited for confirmation from her leaders before beginning her work with the poor and dying people on the streets, and in the dark mines. She worked in a team, never alone. She realized that a servant of the Lord needs boundaries. Her ministry continues to flourish and bear fruit today because she served in community and did not work alone.

Her "love mark" was humility. For her, to be a servant meant to become nothing so that Christ could become everything. Her desire was to become like her Master, who "made Himself nothing and took the form of a servant" (Phil. 2:7). In her words, "I am nothing, that is why God can use me! God is everything!" She had a philosophy of "nothingness". The work was God's work, not hers. She confessed: "My weakness, God's greatness".

At times she was afraid because of her own weakness, but she trusted completely in the greatness of God. Humility is the mark of love, and the most important key in becoming a servant of God.

She paid no attention to either praise or criticism. She was not alarmed when people misunderstood, belittled or rejected her. And she was not impressed when people praised her. She was "independent of either praise or blame". We too must learn this early, because in the servant ministry that many of you are doing or will do, you will have plenty of both! You will be misunderstood and at times you will be praised. But we must always seek to bless others even while we are suffering. Someone spoke about her in these words: "She understood the anguish of the human soul that felt the absence of God, and she yearned to light the light of Christ's love in the 'dark hole' of every heart buried in destitution, loneliness, or rejection."

She was a woman of faith. In her later years, she constantly felt the pain of darkness, of the absence of God, and her inability to subjectively feel His presence. Yet she acted out of pure faith. She understood the true meaning of faith. One of my favorite Bible professors was Dr. John Bright, author of the classic book *The Kingdom of God.* He defined faith in this way: "When we encounter all manner of fear and despair ... here, indeed, we learn what faith really is: not that smug faith which is untroubled by questions because it has never asked any; but that true faith which has asked all the questions and received very few answers, yet has heard the command, Gird up your loins! Do your duty! Remember your calling! Cast yourself forward upon God" (Kingdom of God, Abingdon Press, pp. 119-120). I can think of no one who has exemplified true faith as much as Mother Teresa, servant of the Lord.

Prayer and self-sacrifice were the foundation stones of her ministry. This is the true spirit of servanthood. Our work is our prayer. Only when we do the work that the Lord has given us to do can we ask others to join us in prayer for the ministry. Prayer is sacrifice; we must become men and women of prayer. If we do not spend time in God's Word so that we hear God speak directly in His Word and in prayer, we will have no direction in our ministry. The result will be that we substitute human vision for God's vision, and hinder the effectiveness of the Gospel.

She never looked back. She obeyed her mother; she never let go of Jesus' hand even in the darkest nights of suffering in Calcutta. Her convent offered her the chance to come aside and be protected by its security. But she replied that her security was in God. The paradox of her life was that during her times of spiritual and emotional darkness, when she even felt at times that she did not have faith, her ministry was actually more powerful. She was able to better understand the darkness of the people she served, and her fruit became more abundant. The more she felt the loneliness of separation from her Lover—Jesus, the more her love for Him grew. She was a servant of sacrificial love. And God used her to change a nation.

Mother Teresa's desire was for God to receive all the glory. "For from him" we as servants have received a love that conquers evil and transforms nations; "through Him" we love others as He has loved us; "to Him" alone we give all honor, praise and glory. Amen. (see Romans 11:36)

Hymn for contemplation and Worship

Wondrous Love
John 16; Rom. 3:25; 8:31-32; 1 Pet. 1:1-2; Rev. 12:11

With His own blood, Jesus bought us for the Father.
He redeemed us from the bondage of our sin;
Freed us from our fear of death,
that with ev'ry grateful breath
we would live for Him who died and rose again.

For the Father gave us all to His beloved Son,
and ordained that as He is so shall we be.
Whom He called, He justified,
glorified for Christ a Bride:
wondrously one flesh with Him! What mystery!

Chorus
O, what wondrous love is this?
Called to join the Triune bliss!
O what wondrous love is this?
Wondrous love!

And the Father, for the Son's sake, sent the Spirit.
And the Spirit sanctifies us in the Son:
speaks to us what He has heard,
leads us in the Living Word,
magnifies before our eyes the promised One.

And the Spirit bids us join the deep communion
of the Father, Son, and Spirit—love unknown!
Humbly, we dare to obey,
as through Christ, our living Way,

full assurance draws us to the gracious throne.

<u>Chorus</u>
O, what wondrous love is this?
Called to join the Triune bliss!
O what wondrous love is this?
Wondrous love!

"And they have conquered him by the blood of the Lamb and by the word of their testimony, for they loved not their lives even unto death" Rev. 12:11.

This hymn speaks of the eternal love of the triune God which the church is privileged to mirror in the world. When we fully understand and embrace the wondrous love of our God, we are free and empowered to love others as He would love.

We say Amen to: "It is our absolute response to God's absolute love. Jesus the Servant changed the world. And He promises that those who follow Him and love as He loves will also change the world. We receive the fullness of God's love, grace upon grace; then His love flows through us to the world as we obey His will. The fruit of God's love then returns to our Father in heaven through the praises of those who have received God's love through our lives of service. As servants of God we also have an 'inheritance that is imperishable, undefiled, and unfading, kept in heaven' for us" (1 Pet. 1:4) (David Ross).

Chapter Eight

The Servant of Peace

The Lord told me to be His fool – St. Francis of Assisi

One of the joys of living in the Pacific Northwest is watching the movement of the majestic evergreen trees when they begin to sway in a light wind. It is almost as if they are dancing, with slow, graceful movements not unlike the movement of a Korean classical dance team. Isaiah captured this beauty when he described the return of his captive people from their long exile. "For you shall go out in joy and be led forth in peace; the mountains and the hills before you shall break forth into singing, and all the trees of the field shall clap their hands" (Is. 55:12).

A people who knew no peace would now have peace. The apostle Paul spoke of a deeper peace, a spiritual peace that Christ brought to a whole world in exile. "For He himself is our peace, who has made us both one and has broken down in His flesh the dividing wall of hostility" (Eph. 2:14). Paul was waiting for a hearing in the Roman Emperor's court when he wrote these words. Why was he taken into custody in Jerusalem by Roman troops? Because he was accused of violating the dividing wall of hostility by taking a non-Jewish person into the court of the Jews. This was a real wall, with a sign that read: "No admittance to Gentiles upon penalty of death." Paul did not actually do that, but such a strong accusation caused Jewish people to vow their own lives in order to assassinate Paul. The Romans wanted peace; so they arrested Paul.

One of the greatest examples of racial prejudice in ancient times was the prejudice between Jews and Gentiles. Paul focused on this racial prejudice and even wrote his great classic, *The Letter to the Romans,* to plead with the Christians in Rome to worship together as one body in Christ. The Jewish Christians and the non-Jewish Christians refused to meet together, and Paul emphasized the truth that because we are forgiven and made right with God through the sacrifice of Jesus Christ, we must celebrate our life together in the Body of Christ. Celebration should never be a private thing.

All creation rejoices when people live in peace.

Peace is wholeness, well-being, a "supernaturally natural" contentment that comes when all things are reconciled and united in Christ. The psalmist tells us that the heavens declare the glory of God and His handiwork. All creation celebrates when God's love rules over human sin and divisiveness. The birds of the air sing with joy, even the animals seem to be aware of the change when people around them live in peace.

Yet the world today is broken; most nations are troubled by continuing hostilities, racial prejudice, economic and political oppression. Violence and war are occurring in formerly peaceful areas, anger and fear mark the lives of far too many people. Paul spoke truthfully when he said, *"all creation waits with eager longing for the revealing of the sons of God"* (Rom. 8:19).

God is searching for servants of peace.

Everything a servant of the Lord does relates to peace. When we witness to new life in Jesus Christ, we are promising eternal peace to all who will receive Him by faith. When we work for justice we are seeking to remove the barriers to peace. When we share God's love we are making it possible for people to live in peace. God is searching for a man, or a woman, whose life goal is to bring God's peace to all creation.

God has raised up servants of peace throughout history, but He found one special servant whom we all should consider. We must go back in history to the end of the 12th century and the beginning of the 13th. It was either in late 1181 or early 1182 when Francis of Assisi entered the world. Our purpose here is to go beyond the statue in a garden, with birds sitting on his shoulder, which is the only knowledge most people have of this unique servant of peace. Yes, it is true that birds felt at home resting on his shoulder, and that other animals seemed to be attracted to him because they could sense the peace that emanated from him. He loved the sun and the moon, and sang about them, just as the psalmist did. But his passion was to bring peace both to a broken church and to the violent world of his day.

Francis was born at a time when people were awakening from a deep sleep known as the Dark Ages. Historians speak of the twelfth and thirteenth centuries as "an awakening of the world" from the dark period that began when barbarian tribes crushed the Roman Empire and nearly rid the world of literature and the arts.

But it was not entirely dark. God still had His servants. The Church replaced the Roman Empire as the focus of life; monasteries were founded, ascetic monks went into the desert to pray for God's salvation of the world. Much of the great literature and art of early history was salvaged and protected by these monks living a cloistered life. They taught common people to read and write, and how to grow good crops. But their great calling was to pray. Their lives were committed to purging the world of its pagan roots. God worked through the Dark Ages to cleanse His Church.

Then He brought a young man into the world to complete the renewal of His Church and to bring healing to a world that was escaping the prison of paganism. It is true that new nations were arising, universities were emerging, and the arts were beginning to flourish. But it was a world where urban riots took place daily, where the poor were severely oppressed by the rich, and murders and violence were common.

St. Francis of Assisi is important to us today because we face similar problems. Alexander Solzhenitsyn spoke of the similarities in his commencement address at Harvard University in 1978. He spoke of the present time as a "watershed in history, equal in importance to the turn from the Middle Ages to the Renaissance." This was his challenge: "We shall have to rise to a new level of life where our physical nature will not be cursed as in the Middle Ages, but even more importantly, our spiritual being will not be trampled upon as in the Modern Era."

Francis was born into wealth, his father being one of the richest cloth merchants in Italy. The young man enjoyed his life of ease and luxury; his only goal was to become famous. His mother was French, and Francis once dreamed of becoming a great French poet. It was the time of the Crusades, and young men were being called into service to fight against the Moors of Arabia; Francis had a dream and mistakenly thought God was calling him to become a famous knight. He left his family to become a knight, but on the way he had another dream, and God spoke to him and told him not to go fight in the Crusades but to return home and wait, and He would tell him what to do.

He fell into deep depression. One day as he was riding his horse he saw a man walking along the road coming towards him and immediately recognized him as a leper. Francis was a brave man, afraid of nothing, except leprosy. But without being aware of what he was doing, he jumped down off his horse, rushed to the leper and put his arms around him. He then kissed the leper's hands, gave him some money and mounted his horse to return home. But according to St. Bonaventura, who wrote a biography of St. Francis, when he turned back to look, the leper had disappeared. St. Bonaventura said that the leper was Christ.

Francis would indeed become famous, but as a servant of His Lord, Jesus Christ. One day he went into a small church to pray. The church was nearly falling down, in need of much repair. God spoke to him and called him by his name: "Francis, go repair My house, which is falling in ruins." Francis was completely committed to obeying God. He had given away all of his money, but he begged for money and repaired the church. He continued to repair other old church buildings. But God spoke again and told Francis that He wanted him to rebuild the spiritual Church of his day, which was broken and in much decay.

Someone once remarked that "as Francis had been building churches, so God had been building Francis." I mentioned previously the privilege we had of working with Elder Kim Duk Young, a great woman of God who followed in the footsteps of St. Francis. She and her student disciples decided together that they would build a church on their national university campus. But Mrs. Kim told them, "Before you try to build a church building on this campus, you must first allow God to build His Church in you. You must become radical followers of Jesus and never turn back." This they did, and God miraculously used them to do something that had never been done before. They built a church on the campus of the national university of Korea! Their faithfulness resulted in a great movement of the Holy Spirit on university campuses throughout the nation of Korea.

Throughout his life, Francis was regarded as a fool by both his enemies and even by his closest friends. He fell in love, but his bride was "Lady Poverty." He lived and ministered among the poor, the lepers, the outcasts, but also among the wealthy and leaders of society. Both the poor and the rich began to follow him. When he had no more than a dozen followers, he dared to go to Rome and ask the pope to recognize them as a religious order. God gave the pope a dream at that same time, and the pope recognized their order. Francis' followers continued to grow, and by the close of the thirteenth century his movement was joined by more than 30,000 people.

Francis' goal in life was to be a "fool for Christ," to seek no worldly recognition, to rid his nation of poverty by living and working among the poor, to live a life of prayer and worship along with social reform to show Christians how to live a radical Christian life that would bring renewal and revival to the Church, and to work for the healing of his nation. And all this he did with great joy!

Remember, this was the time of the Crusades, and most Christians believed that all Muslims must be exterminated; Muslims felt the same way about Christians. But Francis wanted the Muslims to share in the blessings of Christ, and he wanted peace between the two religions. He finally received permission from his superior (who called him a fool) to cross enemy lines during the Crusades to meet the Sultan of the Saracens and ask for peace. This "fool for Christ" started out with two companions to convert the Muslim world! Miraculously, Francis was able to meet the Sultan, who refused Francis' invitation to become a Christian but who nevertheless welcomed Francis and even allowed him to visit the Muslim controlled Holy Land before returning to his own people.

A modern day St. Francis among the Muslims was Dr. William McElwee Miller, a remarkable 20th century missionary to Muslims. He had deep friendships with Muslims. Once a mullah, or leader of Muslims, asked Dr. Miller, "What is Christianity?" He answered that it was like a journey, and all he needed was bread for nourishment, water for refreshment, a book for direction, and opportunity for service. The mullah knew that Dr. Miller was talking about the bread of life, the water of the Spirit, the Bible, and service for God. The door was open for genuine dialogue.

This wonderful servant of the Lord visited the theological seminary where I was a student, and I asked him, "Dr. Miller, what is the secret of your ministry to Muslims?" His answer was, "Prayer and worship! Prayer is the breath of the Christian. Worship is the gift of our lives to our Lord, to become His servants." He added that we must have a spirit of humility that shares the gospel of salvation not only through words but also by living a servant life among them. A true servant of peace!

Francis, the "poor man of peace," founded three religious orders. The first was that of the friars, who were monks who did not live in monasteries but walked the streets as troubadours, singing, making joyous melody to the Lord, witnessing by both words and deeds. This order was very strict, insisting on total poverty and trusting the Lord for everything. They showed a "radical alternative" to the ordinary Christian life. The second order was an order for women, led by St. Francis' deep friendship with St. Clare. This friendship was a pure and spiritual friendship, which is unbelievable to those who do not believe that a spiritual friendship can be as real as sexual love. As G.K. Chesterton says, in his classic biography of St. Francis, divine love is the greatest reality. The third order was one of the greatest gifts to the Church of his day. It was an order for all Christians, with guidance for sharing in this great movement without leaving their homes or interrupting their normal life. It enabled many people to live the servant life in the midst of the world. Perhaps this third order is the most needed today.

The Canticle of Brother Sun

Time and space do not permit us to tell of Francis' great appreciation of nature and the environment, his love for all of God's creation, the sun and the moon, the stars and the earth with its great mysteries. He loved all living creatures, the birds, the fish and all animals. He may have been the first Christian environmentalist. Is it not true that a servant of peace must be concerned for the environment as well as for the people who depend on a healthy environment for their welfare?

St. Francis was a poet and singer of the Gospel, a traveling musician and evangelist; but the most important thing about him was that he was a worshiper of God. He loved the Scriptures, and when he taught God's Word the good news seemed to take wings and spread throughout the land.

He loved people; and he is loved by all Christians. What was his secret? He was the Lord's servant of peace whom God used to renew the Church and heal his nation. St. Francis is still not understood by many people today; but is this not true of most servants of the Lord?

Just as each individual is created uniquely by God, so are His servants called to unique service in the world. Out of his love for God's creation, he composed poems of praise and sang them, with the heart of the psalmists. Psalm 148 enables us to know the heart of this servant of God who sang praises, prayed and labored that there may be peace in the earth, the sky, in nations and in all hearts. His most famous poem, *The Canticle of Brother Sun,* echoes this psalm. (See also Ps. 19.)

The Canticle of Brother Sun

Most High, all-powerful, good Lord,
Yours are the praises, the glory, the honor, and all blessing.
To You alone, Most High, do they belong,
and no man is worthy to mention Your name.
Praised be You, my Lord, with all your creatures,
especially Sir Brother Sun,
Who is the day and through whom You give us light.
And he is beautiful and radiant with great splendor;
and bears a likeness of You, Most High One.
Praised be You, my Lord, through Sister Moon and the stars,
in heaven You formed them clear and precious and beautiful.
Praised be You, my Lord, through Brother Wind,
and through the air, cloudy and serene, and every kind of weather
through which You give sustenance to Your creatures.
Praised be You, my Lord, through Sister Water,
which is very useful and humble and precious and chaste.
Praised be You, my Lord, through Brother Fire,
through whom You light the night
and he is beautiful and playful and robust and strong.
Praised be You, my Lord, through our Sister Mother Earth,
who sustains and governs us,
and who produces varied fruits with colored flowers and herbs.
Praised be You, my Lord, through those who give pardon
for Your love
and bear infirmity and tribulation.
Blessed are those who endure in peace

for by You, Most High, they shall be crowned.
Praised be You, my Lord, through our Sister Bodily Death,
from whom no living man can escape.
Woe to those who die in mortal sin.
Blessed are those whom death will find in Your most holy will,
for the second death shall do them no harm.
Praise and bless my Lord and give Him thanks
and serve Him with great humility.

*Recommend reading on St. Francis of Assisi
can be found in Appendix 2.

***The Canticle of Brother Sun* by St. Francis
can be heard on YouTube.

Hymn for Contemplation and Worship

The Wall Brought Down
(Mk. 10:42-45; Eph. 2)

The wondrous cross that saved my soul,
that bore my sin and bought me whole,
a further wonder did achieve,
uniting all those who believe.
The wondrous cross brought down the wall,
stilling the strife between us all.
Now from all flesh, Gentile and Jew,
God forms one body from the two.

Though we are many, we are one.
Each part reflecting God's great Son.
Female and male, servant and free,
bound by one Spirit's unity.
Across the earth, the Church expands.
Saints lift God's praise in distant lands.
While many weep, and suffer loss,
still clinging to the wondrous cross.

Forgive us Lord, the harm we do
when we refuse to follow You.
Forsaking love, we grasp at pow'r.
Come heal our sickness in this hour.
O love amazing, love divine,
transform our hearts, Lord, start with mine!
As we've received, teach us to give,
born in Your love, in love to live.

Text: gap2Theos
Tune: BROKEN WALL Alt: JERUSALEM

As we reflect upon Christ's death on the cross, we should give due attention to the fact that his death is our peace—not only with God but also with one another. Ephesians 2:11-22 is the primary text for such theology. There is clear admonition elsewhere in the Scriptures that the love of God displayed at the cross should provoke us to love one another (1 Jn. 4:10-12).

In the hymn I have written here, I seek to celebrate the horizontal reconciliation that has been gloriously affected by the same cross. As Paul's writing makes clear, however, it is one thing to profess belief in this message, and quite another to obey it. In our contemporary situations, we need to recognize the effects of injustice and pain in our world and offer practical efforts to bring peace and justice and raise people toward well-being.

Mark 10:42-45 – Jesus called them together and said, "You know that those who are regarded as rulers of the Gentiles lord it over them, and their high officials exercise authority over them. Not so with you. Instead, whoever wants to become great among you must be your servant, and whoever wants to be first must be slave of all. For even the Son of Man did not come to be served, but to serve, and to give his life as a ransom for many."

I have written a simple tune for this, which I call BROKEN WALL. The hymn can be sung to other familiar hymn tunes—for example, HAMBURG (which most of us associate with Watts' hymn), or JERUSALEM.

Chapter Nine

The Servant's Community

Indeed our fellowship is with the Father
and with His Son Jesus Christ

(1 John 1:3).

G od's Spirit came like a mighty rushing wind, filling the upper room where the 120 people were praying; tongues of fire rested upon each person, and they were all filled with the Holy Spirit. Immediately the Spirit began to work supernaturally through the servants of the Lord. But as we read the accounts in the Acts of the Apostles, we discover that no one worked alone. Even Peter, who had preferred to work alone, could no longer do anything alone. When he stood up to preach, he "stood with the eleven" other apostles. (Acts 2:14) This does not mean that all the apostles stood beside him; but they stood with him in the Spirit as he preached.

Another thing we often neglect is probably the most important thing that happened in the life of the Church after Pentecost. A new community was born at Pentecost. Paul, perhaps the greatest of the New Testament servants, revealed his need for community when he spoke these seemingly excessive words to the Christians of Philippi: "My brothers and sisters, whom I love and long for, my joy and crown, stand firm thus in the Lord, my beloved" (Phil. 4:1)!

Christian community is supernatural. Later, when the apostle John invited non-believers to join the Christian community, he told them that "our fellowship is with the Father and with His Son Jesus Christ" (1 Jn 1:3). God is a family – Father, Son and Holy Spirit. The Trinity is three Persons who are one. They love one another with selfless love, in perfect unity. God knows that no one can live alone, especially servants of God. So His Spirit baptizes us into a new community that is controlled, guided and overflowing with God's love. He equips His servants to live together in such a way that His love overflows from our lives like a river, for the healing of nations. The psalmist says it best: "Behold, how good and pleasant it is when brothers and sisters dwell in unity! For there the Lord commands the blessing, life forevermore" (Ps. 133:1,3).

The Spirit takes "non-kindreds" and makes us "kindreds," the family of God. We are supernaturally bonded to one another, with Jesus as our Head. The key to Christian community is that we do not meet each other just in the presence of one another; we meet each other in the presence of God! God's presence in each of us is like a magnet that draws us into perfect unity. God Himself is the head of our community. He does not give us the privilege of limiting the members of our community to those we feel close to or enjoy being with. If He had allowed the original disciples to choose who to share their lives with, Matthew, a tax collector, would never have chosen Peter, a quick-tempered fisherman, or Simon the Zealot.

God's community is worldwide.

God is the Father of every nation, people group, and family on earth. His community is international and interracial. The beauty of the Holy Spirit community is that people of all races are united into one family; rich and poor Christians share with one another and teach one another; highly educated Christians and non-educated Christians break bread together. A true community of servants of the Lord does not take pride in boasting of their denominational preferences. In 1978, I had the privilege of visiting the Benedictine Convent of Catholic sisters at the Fatima Hospital in Taegu, Korea. Our time of prayer together revealed the beauty of community in the Holy Spirit. The Mother Superior of the community called me aside and said, "David, we are a community of one hundred and one sisters. One hundred of us are born again in Jesus Christ and have been baptized in the Holy Spirit. Only one sister is holding out and refuses to be filled with the Spirit. Please pray for her." As I prayed with the one hundred and one sisters, asking God for an outpouring of the Holy Spirit on the land of Korea, both North and South, one of the sisters spoke out this brief prophetic word: "Walk into My road; come into My life, and I will cause life to flower around you." Then another sister prayed for me with these words, "Lord, please bless the Presbyterians more than the Catholics!"

When we become Christians, we are immediately bonded together with every other Christian in the world. Every Christian you meet, regardless of their race, their ethnicity, their denominational ties, their economic class or political persuasion, is your brother, your sister, or your mother, your son or daughter. A true servant of God rejoices in this worldwide unity of God's community, which is the Church. Christ is present in His Church. He is present in each of us, and we become the witness of His presence to one another. At times I pause to give thanks for the witnesses in my life who have been the presence of Christ for me.

At a time in the world's history where divisiveness threatens to destroy our civilizations, we who have answered God's call to become His servants to transform the world rejoice that we can walk together in community and be led by the Holy Spirit to accomplish God's purposes in the world.

Christian community is organic.

One of the great teachers on the nature of community was Father Archer Torrey (R. A. Torrey III), the founder of Jesus Abbey in Korea; for many years he continued to open my eyes to understand the New Testament meaning of community. He would always begin by saying, "community is organic". The Church is not an organization, nor is it a movement or denomination or building. It is a living organism, the living body of Christ. Jesus explained what this means by saying, "I am the vine; you are the branches. Abide in Me". When we abide in Him we will bear much fruit. Our relationship with Jesus is an organic, living relationship. We receive life from Him, and that life flows out into the world. The key question for us today is, *are we abiding?* Are we resting in the constant love of Jesus, continuously receiving the inflowing power and strength of His Holy Spirit?

The apostle Paul explained the organic relationship by reminding us that we are the *body of Christ.* Christ is the Head, and we all are members of His Body. We must care for one another just as the body cares for its different parts. If one member of the body suffers, we also suffer. If one member rejoices, we must rejoice with that person. We share our lives together as the family of God. Both of these metaphors are actually statements of a reality. There can be no division. The key question for this metaphor is, *is the body healthy? Are we a growing, life-giving community of the Holy Spirit?* My Norwegian friend Frank Kaleb Jansen traveled the world as a diplomat and entrepreneur. He often was asked what church he belonged to, and his answer was always, "Oh, I am a member of the BOC." Most people did not question him further even though they had no idea what the BOC was; finally a young man asked the question, and Frank smiled as he replied, "I am a member of the Body of Christ".

New Testament community is *koinonia.*

God wants the same kind of community today that He established in the Early Church. The Greek word for *koinonia* or its derivatives appears only 60-62 times in the New Testament. This one small word has many meanings, such as fellowship, or intimacy, responsible relationships, accountability, sharing, being co-workers in the sense of economic cooperation, partners, and more. The root meaning of this word—*koinos*—means "to have in common". But the basic meaning of *koinonia* can be summarized by three basic usages of the word.

Communion – Intimacy with God

Remember the definition of a servant that we spoke of earlier. A servant is one who belongs to God, who loves him without condition; and who stands under the authority of God in absolute obedience, desiring to do His will. The *koinonia* of the Holy Spirit enables a servant to live in a manner true to his calling. Our life begins with communion with God.

A commonly used benediction in churches is taken from 2 Corinthians 13:14. "The grace of the Lord Jesus Christ and the love of God and the communion of the Holy Spirit be with you all." This benediction reveals the nature of each Person of the Trinity: Jesus, the Son, gives us *grace*, the undeserved favor of God; God the Father is *love*, unconditional and unlimited; the Holy Spirit enables all Christians to commune with God, becoming identified with Him in intimate *fellowship*. The fruit of grace and love is *koinonia* – fellowship, or communion with God. When we have fellowship with one another after a worship service, enjoying coffee and doughnuts, or rice cakes and tea, we are celebrating our fellowship, or communion, with one another. The coffee and tea do not create the communion; they are simply a delicious way to celebrate the organic union we have with God and with one another. When we partake of holy communion, we use bread and the fruit of the vine to celebrate our union with God and with one another.

Jesus Christ initiated community when He *identified* with humans by being born as a baby. "Since therefore the children share in flesh and blood, He Himself likewise partook (*meteschen,* a Greek word similar to *koinonia*) of the same things, that through death He might destroy the one who has the power of death, that is, the devil" (Heb. 2:14).

The writer of *Hebrews* pleaded with the Christians who were undergoing severe trials to identify with one another as *partners* (*koinonoi*) in order to strengthen one another. Community is not about living together in one location or merely cooperating with one another to complete our given tasks. It is to *identify* with one another, just as Jesus identified with us by becoming fully human (Heb. 2:14). The power of our life together is that we identify with one another by accepting one another in our loneliness and sufferings as well as in our times of happiness. As I write these words, the whole world is enduring a deadly pandemic; but the greatest disease in the world is not the covid virus; it is the loneliness that comes from disconnected lives. We who are servants of the Lord, in whatever occupation we are engaged, know how deadly loneliness can be. We also know that the only cure for loneliness is *intimacy* with the Lord and with one another, welcoming one another in the name of the Lord. As we share in community with other believers, the Holy Spirit strengthens us by transforming our loneliness into *solitude;* we invite Jesus to come into our loneliness, and discover that He is always with us in our loneliness. We may be lonely, but we are never alone; Jesus shares our loneliness and gives us strength to endure and overcome. This is the heart of *koinonia* community.

Relationship – Sharing and Responsibility

Responsibility is the mark of community. As servants of God, we are responsible to Him; we fulfill our responsibility by obedience, delighting to do His will. In our life together, the Holy Spirit uses our community to bring us closer to Christ and to make us more like Him. The entire New Testament speaks of this aspect of community. The New Testament speaks in a deeply personal way to each one of us, but it is a corporate book, directed toward God's community, the Body of Christ.

Servants share spiritual things. Acts 2:42-47 and 4:32-37 reveal that all members of the community shared the apostles' teaching; they shared their prayer life with one another; they participated together in Holy Communion. They shared the Word with one another, and they worshiped together in joy. This deep spirituality gave them the desire and the power to share their whole lives with one another, so that the unbelievers all around them would say, "Behold, how these Christians love one another!"

We are a covenant community. God's covenant means that God takes full, complete responsibility for His people; in response we obey Him and follow Him wherever He leads. God wants His servants – the people of God – to live in the same covenant relationship with one another. The Christian community in the New Testament was marked by its members' responsibility to and for one another. They were responsible spiritually, and also socially. They were concerned about the moral lives of one another. They took responsibility for one another when a person was in sorrow, or depressed. They took economic responsibility for one another, to the degree that *"there was not a needy person among them!"* (Acts 4:34) This does not mean that the poor were not members of the church; there were no poor in the church because believers shared all things with one another. Theirs was a day-to-day responsible relationship.

In order to have a responsible relationship, each member must be accountable to other members of the community. Accountability means that I give other members of my community the right to speak into my life, to encourage me when I am discouraged. I allow others to comfort me even when I would prefer to be alone, without their comfort. I allow them to discipline me when I go astray. Living responsibly is walking

92

in the light, confessing our sin when we have walked in darkness, and giving and receiving forgiveness.

Making the decision to live in responsible, accountable relationships with other servants of the Lord will be costly, because it will run contrary to our overly private, independent lifestyles. But it can be the turning point of our lives. We begin to minister as a team, and not just as individuals who seek others' help only in time of need.

Taking responsibility for one another and sharing with one another is the power that removes the competitive spirit that still lingers in most churches and mission organizations. Just as spring flowers were beginning to blossom in New York City, where we lived in 1998, I discovered the blossoming of *koinonia* in an unexpected place. All the world knows Yo-Yo Ma, the famous cellist; but probably not as many know of his equally talented sister, Dr. Yeou-Cheng Ma, who was a violin prodigy as a child but later became a developmental pediatrician at the Albert Einstein College of Medicine in the Bronx. The March 11, 1998, edition of the New York Times included an insightful article about the Children's Orchestra Society, a training ground for musicians aged 4 to 18. In order to make it available to all talented students, rich or poor, the tuition is only $450 a year (in 1998). It was founded by her father in 1962 and is directed by Dr. Ma and her husband, Michael Dadap. (www.childrensorch.org)

The uniqueness of this orchestra society is the firm belief in a child's innate capability to learn and develop musical talent of the highest level, *when nurtured in a supportive environment.* Dr. Ma herself spoke of having experienced the "steely competitiveness" of the music world as a child; she herself was healed of those feelings, and now enables the children to use competition as a tool for learning, but not as a goal in performing.

One event in their training program illustrates beautifully the theme of sharing and taking responsibility for one another in community. The orchestra at that time held an annual concerto competition. According to Dr. Ma, the winner "must demonstrate good musical citizenship, be a team player and have good attendance." The outside judges selected a 14-year old Japanese-American violinist, Yumi Sagiuchi, who joined the orchestra when she was seven. She had won two years before, and when the honor came to her again, she deferred to another student! The judges had to select another winner! Everyone was shocked by this spirit of sharing, which created an "infectious sense of empowerment" among the young players, who were heard to remark: "Who needs the London Symphony? We can do it ourselves!"

Hyunmee Lee, who has contributed greatly to this book by her beautiful and powerful renditions of Gary's hymns, once served as Assistant Music Director of their orchestra and directed their summer master class program.

Here is *koinonia* in action: Healing, excellence without destructive competition, caring for one another, taking responsibility for one another; or in the words of the writer of *Hebrews,* "encouraging one another to love and good works." Yes, community—sharing life with one another and living with others responsibly—can change the world! Perhaps this would be a good time to pause from your reading and find another person with whom you can share a "*koinonia* handshake." Paul, Peter, James and John gave one another this "right hand of fellowship (*koinonias*)" when they blessed Paul to continue his witness to the non-Jewish world (Gal. 2:9).

Partnership – Mission to the World

Jesus called two brothers, who were fishermen. His promise was, "Follow Me, and I will make you fishers of men." (Matt. 4:19) They were partners in the fishing business; and Jesus transformed this business partnership into a spiritual, missional partnership, while maintaining the basic principles they had in the fishing business. These two disciples began to share with Jesus in proclaiming the Kingdom of God. This is *koinonia* in action! Christian community is dynamic, not static; always moving forward, sharing in the ministry of Christ. Did not Jesus promise that all who follow Him will do the same works that He did, in obedience to the Father? (Jn 14:12-14) Paul gave thanks to God for the Christians of Philippi and told them that he prayed for them with joy, "because of your partnership (*koinonia*) in the Gospel from the first day until now" (Phil. 1:5). He also spoke of Titus, as his *partner* (*koinonos*) and fellow-worker in the Kingdom of God.

Communities that do not extend beyond their own members cannot survive. We must go beyond ourselves, or we cannot live with ourselves. This is why churches that do not engage in mission to the world become powerless. One of the greatest gifts of the Holy Spirit is the gift of forcing us to go beyond ourselves, to commit to the extending of the Kingdom of God into all the world.

A Day in the Life of a Servant Community

We must live each day that the Lord gives us with great joy and expectation of what God will do in our lives, and how He will use us to bless the world. Dietrich Bonhoeffer, in his valuable book on community (*Life Together*), tells us that we must begin our day by being alone with God; then we must share our day with others; finally we must serve the world together.

The Day Alone. As servants of God, each of us should begin our day by having some time alone with God. Morning is preferable, before the day becomes busy; but you should choose the time that is most suitable to you. God invites us to meet Him in His *Holy Place* (Heb. 4:14-16), where we receive mercy and forgiveness for our sins and grace to begin a new day. Jeremiah tells us that "the steadfast love of the Lord never ceases; His mercies never come to an end; they are new every morning. Great is His faithfulness" (Lam. 3:22-23).

Take some time to read a portion of the Bible; then meditate on one or two verses of Scripture and allow God to speak to you. The Psalms are like "today's manna;" just as God fed His people manna in the wilderness, so He will feed His Word to you, especially in the Psalms. Remember, the Holy Spirit is planting the seeds of God's Word into your innermost being, to strengthen you and equip you for the day ahead. Spend a short time in prayer, remembering to always praise and thank the Lord for His blessings; pray for your own needs, then for the needs of others.

The Day with Others. Share with another person the words that God spoke to you in your time alone with Him. Listen to one another. Share your hopes and your sorrows. Open yourself to others so that you can bear one another's burdens. Remember to encourage one another to love and good deeds. Worship with one another when possible.

Try to discover ways to serve other members of your community in this day that the Lord has given you. Above all, celebrate together! A wise man once said, "if you don't have a reason to celebrate, make one!"

Never forget that God delights in the community of His servants! He listens as those who fear the Lord speak with one another! "They shall be Mine in the day when I make up my treasured possession ... for you who fear My name, the sun of righteousness shall rise with healing in its wings. You shall go out leaping like calves from the stall. And you shall tread down the wicked ... on the day when I act" (Mal. 3:8 – 4:3). Remember that God delights in the community of His servants! He listens as those who fear the Lord speak with one another!

The Day in the World. If you are not able to go into the world of many people, do so in your prayers. You can travel both near and far as you intercede for others. Find ways to go into the world as peacemakers, as those who reconcile and bring healing where there is pain. Proclaim the Gospel of life, through your words and through your life. And work for justice in the world.

Hymn for Contemplation and Worship

Holy Communion / koinonia (κοινωνία) (Jn. 13:1-20, 31-35; Acts 2:42; 1 Co. 10:16; 11:17-34; Phil. 1:5; Heb. 13:16; 2 Pet. 2:12; 1 Jn 4:7-10; Jude 12)

Chorus:
Take and eat, each one of you.
This is My Body given for you (Lk. 22:19).
Take and drink, each one of you.
This is My Blood poured out for you (Lk. 22:20).

Beloved friends, let us each other love (1 Jn. 4:7),
for love is from God and whoever loves
has been born of God and truly knows God.
He who loves not, knows not God, Who is love (1 Jn. 4:8).

The love of God was made manifest (1 Jn. 4:9).
God sent His Son that we might live through Him.
In this is love, not that we have loved God (1 John 4:10),
but God sent His Son to atone for our sins.

I know not how—
for that I first must know Thee.
I know I know Thee not as I would know Thee,
For my heart burns
like theirs that did not know Him,
Till He broke bread,*
and therein they must know Him.

Here is my heart—
from Thine, Lord, fill it up,
That I may offer it as the holy cup

of Thy communion to my every man.
May we Your Body in this faith always stand.

Chorus
Take and eat, each one of you.
This is My Body given for you (Lk. 22:19).
Take and drink, each one of you.
This is My Blood poured out for you (Lk. 22:20).

May our koinonia with one another reflect our koinonia with our Lord Jesus.

"Dear friends, let us love one another, for love comes from God. Everyone who loves has been born of God and knows God. Whoever does not love does not know God, because God is love. This is how God showed his love among us: He sent his one and only Son into the world that we might live through him. This is love: not that we loved God, but that he loved us and sent his Son as an atoning sacrifice for our sins. Dear friends, since God so loved us, we also ought to love one another. No one has ever seen God; but if we love one another, God lives in us and his love is made complete in us" 1 John 4:7-12.

"As often as you eat this bread and drink this cup, you proclaim the Lord's death till he comes" (1 Cor. 11:26).

*Last two verses were adapted from George MacDonald in *A Diary of Lost Souls*, 11/20 & 6/1.

Chapter Ten

The Hidden Servant

"For you have died, and your life is hidden with Christ in God"
(Col. 3:3).

The most important thing the prophet Elijah learned in hiddenness was God's timing. He is never too early, and never too late. He allowed Elijah to minister at the exact time He had prepared for him to confront King Ahab.

We can begin by obeying the words of 1 Peter 5:6 – "Humble yourselves, therefore, under the mighty hand of God so that at the proper time He may exalt you." It's all about timing; we must be ready when God decides it is the right time to use us to bear the most fruit.

A common weakness among servants is the temptation to be overly busy with completing the work the Lord has given us to do. Time passes so quickly; there are so many things to do. Once when the crowds were coming and going, and there was no time even to eat, Jesus observed a similar agitation and restlessness in His disciples; so He said to them, "Come aside by yourselves to a secluded place and rest a while" (Mark 6:31 NASB). We can hear the disciples murmuring to one another: "Does He think we have time to rest when we should be working harder? We can never hide from these crowds." But they got into a boat and went with Jesus to a deserted place, only to discover even greater crowds waiting there for them. One of the disciples probably muttered the words "no rest for the weary".

Jesus never sought rest as a way to avoid people; on the contrary, He saw the great crowds and had compassion on them, "because they were like sheep without a shepherd" (Mark 6:34). Jesus was not speaking to His disciples only about physical rest, though this is important, and we must take time to rest our tired bodies. He was simply telling His disciples to come home.

But where was home for these busy disciples? Where is home for God's busy servants today? We know the answer: "For you have died, and your life is hidden with Christ in God" (Col. 3:3). Hiddenness is the Christian's home.

The Power of Hiddenness

Here is one of the paradoxes of the Christian. Paul explains the paradox. We are dead but very much alive; we have died to sin and to the "elemental (evil) spirits of the world," in order that sin might have no control over us (Rom. 6:1-7; Colossians 3:3). Our life is hidden with Christ in God. Heaven is already here!

"He who dwells in the secret place of the Most High shall abide under the shadow of the Almighty" (Ps. 91:1 NKJV). The Lord Himself has always been our dwelling place in all generations (Ps. 90:1). The "secret place of the Most High" is where all ministry is given birth; it is where Christ works in us and through us by the power of His Spirit.

Isaiah speaks of this power of hiddenness in the second Suffering Servant Song (Is. 49:1-7). Hiddenness is one of the gifts God gives to His servants. "He made my mouth like a sharp sword; in the shadow of His hand He hid me; He made me a polished arrow; in His quiver He hid me away." Hiding in God, or being hidden in Him, is not passive; it is rather the most dynamic place for a servant. For this is where all ministry is given birth. What happens when God hides us? We will understand more fully when we examine the Scriptures to see how God hid many of His servants, and understand His reasons for hiding them.

Finding Rest in Hiddenness

When Jesus told His disciples to come apart to a quiet place and rest awhile, He was teaching them that all ministry begins with resting in God. The Letter to the Hebrews explains this rest (Hebrews chapter 4); we rest in God's presence by ceasing to work "for God," and allowing God to work through us by the power of His Holy Spirit. The apostle Paul knew where his home was; so he could confess, "I worked harder than any of them, though it was not I, but the grace of God that is with me" (1 Cor. 15:10). Servants work hard and become tired physically, emotionally and even intellectually; but we must not become tired spiritually by refusing to allow the Spirit to work through us. Many are the servants who have worked hard to the point of exhaustion; such was the case of the servant in Isaiah 49. The four Suffering Songs point to Jesus Christ as the Servant; yet God was calling all Israel to become His servants to bless the world. These servants were complaining (just as many Christians complain today), saying, "We have labored in vain, spent our strength for nothing and vanity" (Is. 49:4). Jesus calls all His servants to come apart with Him and rest awhile until we are able to allow Him to be our strength; and until we can rejoice that our life is hidden with Christ in God.

Empowered by the Word in Hiddenness

When we find rest in hiddenness, we also discover our greatest weapon for overcoming the Enemy and our tool for completing the work God has given us to do. God has given the servant His Word to proclaim to the world: a sharp sword to penetrate the hardest mind, a polished arrow to soar to the ends of the earth (Is. 49:2). For the Word to be effective in accomplishing God's purpose for sending it, we must be hidden in the Word until we are controlled by the Word. Isaiah explains these words later, in Isaiah 51:16 – "I have put My words in your mouth and covered you with the shadow of my hand."

The Word of God is a seed (Luke 8:11). God hides us in His Word, and His Spirit hides God's Word in us. A seed likes to be hidden, planted in the dark soil; otherwise it will not bring new life. In the same way, God's Word must be hidden in our hearts until our minds are transformed and shaped by the Word of God. Then it will bring forth much fruit in the servant's life.

A seed needs time to generate life; so also God's Word needs time to rest in you so that you might obey His Word and proclaim it with authority. Ask God to hide you in His Word. He will do so as you "let the Word of Christ dwell in you richly" (Col. 3:16), especially through meditation and prayerful reading. God's purpose in hiding you in His Word is to transform you by renewing your mind so that your mind and thoughts will be shaped by His truth that abides in you. You will become a man or woman of the Word; God's Word will comfort and strengthen you, give you wisdom and power.

Servants of God who undergo great persecution have testified time and time again of the power of God's Word hidden within them that enabled them to survive and even flourish in times of trouble.

Christians in China had a special word already hidden in their hearts when the communists took control in 1950. Many of them have spoken of God's promise in Jeremiah 17:7-8 (NRSV) – "Blessed are those who trust in the Lord, whose trust is the Lord. They shall be like a tree planted by water, sending out its roots by the stream. It shall not fear when heat comes, and its leaves shall stay green; in the year of drought it is not anxious, and it does not cease to bear fruit." The Chinese Church continued to bear fruit in the "years of drought," or persecution. The Suffering Churches all have attested to this truth. Nothing can stop the Word of God.

Rejoicing in Hiddenness

The two greatest servants mentioned in the Bible are 75 years old Abraham and 13 to 15 years old Mary. Abraham believed God when He gave the promise: "I will make of you a great nation" (Gen. 12:2). Abraham trusted against common sense, broke away from the status quo and followed God. "Not knowing where he was to go," he surrendered unconditionally to God. His life was hidden in God.

But the most precious words ever spoken by a servant are the words of young Mary: "Behold, I am the servant of the Lord; let it be to me according to your word" (Luke 1:38). She was troubled by the angel's words; she must have felt very much alone, but she remained serene. Both Mary and Abraham responded as only servants can do, in total trust and surrender. Notice that Mary even responded in the passive verb form; not "I will do it," but simply making herself available to all that God would do: "Let it be to me according to your word." The verb form was passive, but her submission was active. She was allowing God's Word to work powerfully in her life to change the world.

Shortly after this, Mary visited Elizabeth, who was also with child, and remained "hidden" with her for about three months. Elizabeth's greeting was, "Blessed are you because you believed." Great things happened during this time of the two mothers' hiddenness. John leaped for joy in his mother's womb and both he and his mother were filled with the Holy Spirit! Hiddenness was for them a unique and precious time of worship to the Lord.

Mary burst into her song of praise, "My soul magnifies the Lord, and my spirit rejoices in God my Savior ... for He who is mighty has done great things for me, and holy is His name" (Luke 1:46-55)! This song reveals young Mary's intimacy with God and the great knowledge and wisdom that He had already given her, to prepare her to become the mother of His Son. Would it not be a blessing if God granted you a "time of hiddenness" to praise and worship the Lord?

Character Change in Hiddenness

God is more interested in our character than our human abilities or strength. God used Moses to deliver His people from slavery in Egypt in order to found a new nation, but only after hiding him for forty years in the wilderness to root out his pride and replace it with two character traits of His Son, Jesus: humility and meekness (perfect submission to God's will). Moses had been prepared to deliver his people with his own strength; so God allowed him to fail miserably and completely, then taught him to become nothing so that God could become everything in his life. Moses learned God's vision when he laid down his own.

Jesus chose Peter to become the leader of the Early Church. Of course Jesus knew that Peter was a man of great pride and self-assurance. But Jesus had plans to teach Peter humility and meekness. These two character traits are of supreme importance to a servant because they teach the full truth of our dependence upon God and our obedience to His will. How did God instill humility and meekness in Peter? By allowing him to go through a time of darkness and hiddenness. Jesus broke Peter's pride by allowing Satan to "sift him like wheat" (Luke 22:31-34), so that he could become a man of character who could "strengthen his brothers."

The clearest example of God's producing character change through hiddenness is Joseph. God hid Joseph for thirteen years, much of that time spent in an Egyptian prison for a crime he did not commit. But God blessed him during his imprisonment by completely changing his character, from a person seeking revenge and competition with his brothers to a man of compassion; from a man with a great hatred to a man of great forgiveness. After Joseph submitted to God's discipline, God endowed him with greater knowledge and wisdom and exalted him to a high position and used him to rescue Egypt and other nations from starvation. And he brought unity and wholeness to his own broken family.

Every servant of God desires to be useful to Him; but we must first be broken of our pride and human self-sufficiency. We are complete only in Him, and we welcome His Spirit who comes to hide us in the grace and mercy of God. Fanny Crosby expressed it well in her hymn:

A wonderful Savior is Jesus my Lord;

he taketh my burden away.

He holdeth me up, and I shall not be moved;

he giveth me strength as my day.

Refrain

He hideth my soul in the cleft of the rock

that shadows a dry, thirsty land.

He hideth my life in the depths of his love,

and covers me there with his hand,

and covers me there with his hand.

Learning God's Principles in Hiddenness

God called Elijah at a time of Israel's great national crisis, during the reign of the wicked king Ahab. The crisis became more severe when Ahab married Jezebel, daughter of the king of Sidon, whose religion was Baal worship. She persuaded Ahab to worship Baal rather than the LORD. Baal worship soon became an openly militant force that threatened to destroy the very fabric of Israel's life and worship of God. Enter Elijah! He was a "God-conscious" man of God with a great sense of mission, eager to begin the great work of saving his nation.

But the word of the Lord came to Elijah. God's first words were, "Arise, depart from here and hide yourself by the brook Cherith" (1 Kin. 17:9)! The Lord placed Elijah in hiding before He allowed him to begin his public ministry. How did God work in Elijah's life during this time of hiddenness?

God was protecting Elijah. But there was something else the Lord was doing: He was teaching Elijah two basic principles of ministry: the flow of ministry and the provision of God.

We must learn the balance, or flow of ministry. We go out to minister in faith, boldly, with the authority that God gives us; but then we come back home again, into the presence of the Lord. We are secure. True security is not the absence of danger; rather, it is the presence of God in us. Knowing the flow of ministry, when to withdraw and when to engage, is the secret of spiritual authority, and of power in ministry. The servant knows that his true home is the presence of God.

The second principle Elijah had to learn was the direct and indirect provision of God. God provided Elijah's needs directly by the brook Cherith, using ravens to feed him. Elijah needed this sign from God as he was beginning his ministry. God would take care of him! Soon after, God provided his needs indirectly, through the widow of Zarephath (1 Kin. 17:2-24). The widow had received no vision that a prophet would come, so she must have been shocked when Elijah asked her for her last supply of food. Mother Teresa spoke often about the generosity of the poor who surrounded her. She said that God often surrounds us by poor, broken and destitute people in order to minister to our needs through them. Regardless of how God supplies our needs, the servant of the Lord wakes up each morning praising God and thanking Him for His provision and care.

Three years later God said to Elijah, "Go, show yourself to Ahab" (1 Kin. 18:1). King Ahab would now know that Elijah had been in the presence of God. The second Suffering Servant Song sings about this, in Isaiah 49:7. "Thus says the Lord, the Redeemer of Israel and His Holy One, to one deeply despised, abhorred by the nation, the servant of rulers: Kings shall see and arise; princes, and they shall prostrate themselves; because of the Lord, who is faithful, the Holy One of Israel, who has chosen you."

Elijah made a remarkable discovery on his way to meet King Ahab. He met Obadiah, another servant of God! God had hidden this believer in the king's palace and had even given him authority over all the king's household matters! Obadiah had actually hidden and fed one hundred of the Lord's prophets, and prevented them from being killed. Wherever you go as God's servant, even in lands where believers are massacred, you may meet these "hidden servants" whom God has planted to prepare the nations for revival. But it is more likely that you will not meet them, because God has hidden them.

Learning to Pray in Hiddenness

God hides His servants for many other reasons. God hides us to protect us; to embrace us in His healing love in times of sickness and infirmity; to cleanse us from sins that we have not been able to conquer; to reveal to us an intimacy with Him that we had not known before, by "speaking tenderly to us" and transforming our previous valleys of suffering or rebellion into doors of hope (Hos. 2:14-15). You will experience many of these blessings in your life as a servant of the Lord, and will be thankful for your times of hiddenness. And you will discover the depth and height, the length and width of His love that you could have come to know in no other way. Often God hides His servants when He calls them to a new ministry, to prepare them to do His will.

But a special gift that God often gives, or increases, in times of hiddenness is the gift of teaching us how to pray. Many powerful servant intercessors have received their calling and anointing while they were hidden because of illness or other forms of suffering. Such was the case of a servant of the Lord whose prayer life was greatly enriched through the hiddenness of suffering for twenty-three years in Soviet prisons and labor camps of Siberia. You can read his story in his book *He Leadeth Me* (Walter J. Ciszek, S.J., Ignatius Press, San Francisco, 1995). Walter Ciszek (1904-1984) was a Polish-American Jesuit priest.

Five of those years were in the infamous Lubianka prison, where he spent 24 hours of the day in solitude in a small, whitewashed room with no furniture except an iron bed. He was permitted to leave only for a twenty minute exercise period and twice daily trips to the toilet. His time there was spent in absolute silence, except for the times of inter-rogation, some of which lasted 48 hours. The absolute silence drove many of the prisoners insane, overcome by their feelings of absolute hopelessness and powerlessness. Fr. Ciszek survived, only to be sen-tenced to 15 more years of hard labor in the Siberian labor camps. Most of those who entered these salt mine labor camps did not come out alive. But he was miraculously freed in 1963 in a prisoner exchange.

Fr. Ciszek discovered that his two decades of hiddenness became for him a "school of prayer." The Lord's Prayer became his source of life. This is how he described it.

> *Jesus begins by placing us in the presence of God: God the almighty, who has created all things out of noth-ingness and keeps them in existence lest they return to nothingness, who rules all things and governs all things in the heavens and on earth according to the designs of His own providence. And yet the same all-powerful God is our Father, who cherishes us and looks after us as His sons [and daughters], who provides for us in His own loving kindness, who guides us in His wisdom, who watches over us daily to shelter us from harm, to provide us food, and to receive us back with open arms when we, like the prodigal, have wasted our inheritance. Even as a father guards his children, He guards us from*

evil—because evil does exist in the world. And just as He can find it in His Father's heart to pardon us, He expects us to imitate Him in pardoning His other sons and daughters, no matter what their offenses.

The Lord's Prayer is a prayer of praise and thanks-giving, a prayer of petition and of reparation ... it is a prayer for all times, for every occasion. It is at once the most simple of prayers and the most profound ... if one could only translate each of its phrases into the actions of his daily life, then he would indeed be perfect as His heavenly Father clearly wishes him to be. Truly, the Lord's Prayer is the beginning and end of all prayers, the key to every other form of prayer.

If we could constantly live in the realization that we are sons of a heavenly Father, that we are always in His sight and play in His creation, then all our thoughts and our every action would be a prayer ... And every true prayer begins precisely here: placing oneself in the presence of God. (pp. 54-63)

He confessed that he did not find it easy to pray – "weak from hunger, weary and pained after long hours of interrogation, distracted by doubts and growing fears for the future, overcome by anxieties induced by constant separation and loneliness, I had to learn to turn to God as best I could and when I could. I had to learn to find Him in the midst of trials as well as nerve-wracking silences, to discover Him and find Him behind all these happenings ... and to ask at every moment for His constant, fatherly protection against the evils that seemed to surround me on all sides." He discovered that his hiddenness was not punishment from God; rather it was the joy of renewed prayer in God's presence.

Receiving Revelation in Hiddenness

God reveals Himself to His servants in hiddenness. Those who are hidden in God's Word testify to a deeper understanding of God's truth revealed in Holy Scripture. Through times of deep communion with the Lord, we come to know Him more fully and love Him more dearly. But there was one man, known as "the disciple whom Jesus loved," who actually received divine revelation of the culmination of history while being hidden as a prisoner of the Roman Empire, on the island of Patmos. The Revelation to John, which is the last book of the Bible, was given to him directly by Jesus Christ, through His angels. John wrote down everything he heard, and today we have the Book of Revelation.

Don't waste your times of hiddenness. Allow God to hide you in His Word. Take comfort in God's promise that nothing can ever separate you from the love of God in Christ Jesus. Maintain your conversational relationship with God, even in times of suffering; for this is the heart of the servant life.

Hymn for Contemplation and Worship

Follow Your Lord (Mt. 16:24; Luke 9:23)
I see through your eyes and into your mind,
I see in your heart. I know where you are.
I know what you're feeling.
The song that I gave, you've left it behind.
For too many days I've been out of your mind.
But now you've been thinking.

Chorus
I laid down My life to open this door.
So come now, My child, and claim your reward.
Come now, My child, and follow your Lord.

The path that you walk, I've been there before.
I laid out the Way, and I opened the door,
So you could come with Me.
Just take up the cross that I gave to you.
Step out in faith, and I'll see you through.
I'll give you the victory.

Chorus
I laid down My life to open this door.
So come now, My child, and claim your reward.
Come now, My child, and follow your Lord.

I wrote this song just before graduating with my Master of Divinity degree in 1983. When I first became a Christian as a high school student, I felt that God was calling me to full time ministry. I, thus, set my future educational and personal trajectory to that goal and was very close to accomplishing it. As I approached my graduation, after all the effort and sacrifices my wife and I had made, I realized that the love and the zeal I had for God when I began the journey was blurred and had grown cold. I felt empty inside and very unworthy to serve God, the Church or anyone else.

As I went through many days of agonizing soul searching and reflection, the words of this song came to me. Jesus was speaking to me that He knows me through and through and all I have to do is to "pick up that cross and follow" my Lord. So the "I" here is the Lord Jesus Christ, and He is speaking to me. I wasn't worthy to be His servant, never was and never will be. The call on my life is not to do great things for God in my strength and effort but to be "hidden" in His work on the cross and simply follow the path He opens up for me.

Following the seminary graduation, in my and my wife's lives, there have been many seasons of "hiddenness" of which David Ross speaks. We paused for two years after the graduation, going back to part-time jobs and not seeking any full time ministry opportunities, simply learning to live each day waiting on and obeying the Lord to open the right door. In 2010, as I experienced a severe traumatic brain injury which stripped off my position and a platform to do ministry, God has "hidden" me to Himself to teach the same truth: that all I am called to do is to daily "take up that cross that I gave to you, and follow your Lord!"

Then He said to them all: "Whoever wants to be My disciple must deny himself and take up his cross daily and follow Me" (Lk. 9:23).

"And whoever does not carry their cross and follow Me cannot be My disciple" (Lk. 14:27).

"Whoever does not take up their cross and follow Me is not worthy of Me" (Mt. 10:38).

Then Jesus said to his disciples, "Whoever wants to be my disciple must deny themselves and take up their cross and follow me" (Mt. 16:24).

Chapter Eleven

The Paradox of Servant Ministry

Having nothing, yet possessing everything
(2 Cor. 6:10)

W e have spoken of hiddenness as one of the paradoxes of the servant. The Holy Spirit, who himself is the "hidden member of the Trinity," reveals this paradox. Jesus expressed this truth to Nicodemus by saying, "The wind (*pneuma*, meaning breath, wind, or Spirit) blows where it wishes, and you hear its sound, but you do not know where it comes from or where it goes. So it is with everyone who is born of the Spirit" (John 3:8). Unseen, yet the Spirit brings new life. He was also unseen at Pentecost; yet the mighty wind and tongues of fire empowered the disciples to proclaim the Gospel of Jesus Christ that overcomes the world!

The Bible is full of paradoxes, as is the life of a servant of God. Have you not wondered at times when you felt especially weak and vulnerable, that God worked most powerfully through you? Perhaps in a time of prayer, when you have reached the extremity of your feelings of helplessness, you are overcome with confidence that nothing is impossible with God. And you rise up with faith that can move mountains.

Yes, it is true. Having nothing, we possess everything. We are sorrowful, yet we rejoice. King David was a servant leader; yet when he first began to gather people around him, he chose the weakest people—I call them the "3 d's": They all were in distress, debt and discontentment (1 Sam. 22:2). Yet they grew to become exceptionally strong leaders; in the words of Ittai, one of his great warriors, "In life or death, there will your servant be" (2 Sam. 15:21).

The Apostle Paul spoke of the paradoxes of the servant of the Lord, in his letter to the Corinthian Christians: "Through honor and dishonor; through slander and praise; treated as imposters yet we are true; as unknown, and yet well known; as dying, and behold, we live; as sorrowful, yet always rejoicing; as poor, yet making many rich; as having nothing, yet possessing everything" (2 Cor. 6:8-10). These paradoxes are but the reflection of God Himself, who is unseen, yet seen by all who love Him. The psalmist comforts us by telling us that "the upright shall behold His face" (Psalm11:7). The Apostle Peter saw the Lord at Pentecost, when the Spirit descended to reveal Him; and he quoted the words of King David to the crowds: "I saw the LORD who is always before me, for He is at my right hand that I may not be shaken" (Acts 2:25). Let's examine some of these paradoxes and discover their power in the life of a servant of the Lord.

Unseen, Yet Seen

The Holy Spirit works in hiddenness to bring new life, like a gentle breeze; or at Pentecost, like a mighty wind; but He is seen by all who walk in His power. Some years ago we were speaking with Fern Noble, a friend and a remarkable servant of God. As a First Nations (or Native American) person, she was talking about how White people, in particular, often do not even see her when she walks into a store. Her people are seemingly invisible in a predominantly White culture that chooses not to see them. I am reminded of something young Amanda Gorman, America's poet laureate, recently said when she was being awarded a high honor. She remarked that she refused to be seen alone, but would only be seen together with all of the young Black women who remain unseen.

Racial issues are not the only reason some people remain unseen. People with power often do not want to see powerless people. We were aware of that when we went with Fern to speak to the people of Kwangju, Korea, on an anniversary of the massacre of hundreds or more young people by military forces in 1980. Families of the deceased, along with great numbers of the citizens of the city, gathered to hear this Native American servant-ambassador speak words of comfort. She identified with their suffering in a way I could not. She spoke to them of God's love and power to use them as His "unseen servants" to bring healing not only to Kwangju but to the whole Korean Peninsula, North and South.

In our ministry together with young people who have escaped from communist North Korea and who are beginning to bless South Korea in many ways, we have seen again the power of being "unseen, yet seen" that God has given to His servants. Missionaries throughout the world live this paradoxical lifestyle as they continue to bless nations with the Gospel of the Kingdom.

If you choose this dangerous privilege of becoming a servant of the Lord, there will be times when God hides you. He may do this to protect you from the many temptations that accompany becoming too well known, or from other dangers; or He may hide you to allow you to grow into the likeness of His Son. But He will use you greatly, and He will receive all the glory.

Poor, Yet Making Many Rich

The apostle Paul spoke of the churches of Macedonia, of which the Philippian Church was the most well-known. "We want you to know, brothers and sisters, about the grace of God that has been given among the churches of Macedonia, for in a severe test of affliction, their abundance of joy and their extreme poverty have overflowed in a wealth of generosity on their part" (2 Cor. 8:1-2). He continued to tell how they gave beyond their means for the favor of taking part in sharing with others in need.

Paul continued to explain how these Christians became so generous. "It did not happen in the way we expected," he said. "Instead they made a complete dedication of themselves first to the Lord and then to us, as God's appointed ministers" (2 Cor. 8:5 J. B. Phillips translation). This is the promise: "Whoever sows bountifully will also reap bountifully ... and God is able to make all grace abound to you, so that having all sufficiency in all things at all times, you may abound in every good work" (2 Cor. 9:6,8).

Generosity is one of the key virtues that people notice among servants of God. It is not a matter of whether one is rich or poor; it is a matter of the heart. But the paradox is the great generosity of the poor. I discovered this gift in a young Indonesian student in a discipleship training school where I once taught. At the end of the week's teaching, she quietly slipped me an envelope. Just before I left to board my flight home from the Jakarta airport, I opened it and found a gift of money from the very student who was suffering the most financial difficulties. When I tried to return it, her only reply was "please don't take this privilege from me." She later became one of the leaders where she ministered.

If you will take some time and read meditatively through Paul's brief Letter to the Philippians, you will discover how this paradox of "having nothing, yet having everything" is an important key that will open the floodgates of blessing to the nations. Ask a missionary; they will tell you about the power of this paradox.

Sorrowful, Yet Always Rejoicing

The last of the four Suffering Servant songs introduces this paradox. This is a song about the crucifixion and resurrection of Christ the Servant. He introduces the song with these words: "Behold, My servant will prosper, He will be high and lifted up, and greatly exalted ... His appearance was marred more than any man, and His form more than the sons of men ... He has no stately form or majesty that we should look upon Him ... a man of sorrows, and acquainted with grief" (Is. 52:13 – 53:3). It is significant that Isaiah spoke first about the resurrection, and only then described the suffering of the cross. We are "resurrection people," and the joy of the Lord is our strength. We suffer with Christ, but we also rejoice with Him.

All servants of the Lord experience sorrow; what makes them different is they rejoice in the midst of sorrow. It happened many times, but once when the apostles were beaten for speaking in the name of Jesus they went on their way "rejoicing that they were counted worthy to suffer dishonor for the name of Jesus" (Acts 5:41)! The stories are too numerous to tell them all. Paul and Silas were beaten mercilessly for delivering a young woman from demon possession; then they were put in chains in the worst section of the prison. But at midnight all the prisoners and guards were astounded when Paul and Silas began to praise and sing loudly hymns of God! God caused an earthquake, and the prison doors flew open! The jailer and his family were saved!

Here is the power of rejoicing in the midst of suffering: God makes His home in the praises of His people (Ps. 22:3). He is enthroned on our praises. St. Teresa of Avila once prayed, "From long-faced saints, deliver us, O Lord." But a careful reading of the Scripture accounts reveal that rejoicing in the Lord often carries with it a "nevertheless." "Nevertheless," said the prophet Habakkuk as he was facing the imminent destruction of his nation, when all of the fields yielded no fruit and they were facing starvation, "I will rejoice in the Lord; I will take joy in the God of my salvation" (Hab. 3:17-18)! That sounds good for characters in the Bible to say, but does it happen today? Perhaps you should ask the lady who fled starvation in her homeland of North Korea, only to be sold into sexual slavery in China, finally to face prejudice in South Korea, if it is unrealistic to rejoice in suffering. She was learning to meditate, and her assignment was to meditate briefly on these two verses from Habakkuk (3:17-18). She quietly read the Scripture; but when she came to the words "yet I will rejoice in the Lord!" she felt deeply wounded and confused. But she continued, and asked the Lord to give her understanding. She was overwhelmed when the Lord appeared to her and enabled her to understand that He had been walking with her as His Shepherd, and that He loved her and had delivered her from destruction; so she decided to obey God. "Yes, Lord, You are my salvation. I have suffered greatly; nevertheless I will rejoice in You." The moment she spoke these words, she was freed from her bondage of despair and hatred. She has continued for many years to find the joy of the Lord in the midst of her pain.

We are living in difficult times, marked by suffering. As Christians we are called to serve the world. We suffer, just as the people of the world suffer. The reasons are many: war, persecution, sickness, financial crisis, loss of loved ones, isolation and many others. How do we rejoice in such a world as this? By finding our strength in the love of the one who suffered for all the sins of the world, yet found His strength to endure the cross "through the joy that was set before Him" (Heb. 12:2). Elisabeth Elliot, whose husband was murdered by the people to whom he was trying to witness, gave us these words of comfort and challenge. "It was a long time before I came to the realization that it is in our acceptance of what is given [whatever that might be], that God gives Himself. This grief, this sorrow, this total loss that empties my hands and breaks my heart, I may, if I will, accept, and by accepting it, I find in my hands something to offer. And so I give it back to Him, who in mysterious exchange gives Himself to me." (Elisabeth Elliot Archives, *Embrace the Trial* – Part 4, posted on September 12, 2017)

Weak, Yet Strong

The apostle Paul and those who ministered with him lived out these paradoxes of servant ministry. He faced slander and rejection, hunger, loneliness and persecution; but he was able to overcome them because he realized that it was actually the Risen Lord who lived in him and worked through him by the power of His Holy Spirit. He was "standing in grace, rejoicing in the hope of the glory of God," as he told the Christians in Rome (Rom. 5:1-2).

Perhaps the key to all of the paradoxes is Paul's confession in 2 Corinthians 12:10: "When I am weak, then I am strong." He could easily have become conceited because of the greatness of the revelations that God gave to him. God even gave him a "thorn in the flesh" to keep him humble; then He told Paul the great secret of servant ministry: "My grace is sufficient for you, for my power is made perfect in weakness." Paul responded by confessing that he would boast more gladly of his weakness, "so that the power of Christ may rest upon me" (2 Cor. 12:9).

Paul worked hard but confessed that it was Christ in Him who was working. He rested in the finished work of Christ and allowed the Holy Spirit to guide and work through Him to the glory of God.

When Paul first spoke about the sufferings and paradoxes of servant ministry, he mentioned some very specific gifts that the Holy Spirit gives His servants (2 Cor. 6:6-7). *Purity* – purity of life and motive; single-minded in serving the Lord and others; *knowledge* – knowing the saving truth revealed in Christ and making the knowledge of Jesus Christ his one goal in life; *patience* – waiting on God, being patient with others, so that all may live in unity; *kindness* – bearing with others, being merciful and compassionate; *the Holy Spirit* – here Paul is probably thinking of the presence of the Spirit in his life who brings holiness, and who continues to strengthen his innermost being and to guide him in the ways of God; *genuine love* – love that is pure and sincere, not hypocritical, and which binds all believers together; *truthful speech* – the truth of the Gospel and truthfulness of his own words; *the power of God* – the supernatural power of God's Holy Spirit which is given only to those who are poor in spirit and do not attempt to minister in their own strength; *the weapons of righteousness* – God's weapons that are not of the flesh but have divine power to destroy Satan's strongholds (2

Cor. 10:3-4); the weapons are both in the right hand and the left hand, to enable us to meet and overcome the enemy from all directions.

These nine gifts are often overlooked when we speak of the sufferings and paradoxes of the servant. But they are given to all who are willing to be weak so that God may be strong in us. As you become more aware of the paradox of your ministry as a servant of the Lord, you will discover that your life is truly hidden with Christ in God. And you will understand why many people cannot understand the way you are living and the risks you are taking. Your life can be explained only by the Holy Spirit.

Hymn for Contemplation and Worship

Like a Well-Weaned Child / Psalm 131

My heart is not proud, O LORD.
My eyes are not haughty.
I do not concern myself with things
too high for me.

But I have stilled and calmed my soul,
like a well-weaned child.
Like a well-weaned child with its mother is my soul.

O, Israel, hope in the LORD.
Hope in the LORD alone, forevermore.

A weaned child is one who has just grown past the time of feeding at its mother's breast. A weaned child no longer can go to its mother's breast for milk. When this happens most children go through a difficult time of adjustment, for they cannot be certain of their mother's response to their demands. They are confused by their mother's apparent separation from them, and they often become fearful and anxious. They may even feel abandoned by their mother.

A well-weaned child is one who has finally learned to trust in the mother's love. For it knows that the mother's love is unchanged and that she will provide for its needs. Now, the child no longer comes to mother's breast for milk ... but continues to come to her for love and comfort, with confidence in her embrace.

As a professor I was expected to give good and logical answers to the questions students ask, and I prided myself that I was quite good at it. After the brain injury, I tried to come up with answers that made sense to the why questions of my life. I went through all the sins great and small in my entire life and tried to see the reasons why I am left with a half the man I once was.

I was obsessed with this and went into a deep depression that led me to a mental breakdown. "When I try to understand all this, it troubled me deeply till I entered the sanctuary of God" (Ps. 73:16-17a).

Just like a weaned child in its mother's embrace, leaving all "that is too high for me," to the Lord. I then began to understand that God's love and calling on me have not changed. It was always about God and not about how good or bad I am. Now that I am left so small and needy it's easier for me to take the eyes off of what I am and what I do to only "enter the sanctuary of God to gaze upon His beauty" (Ps. 27:4). Like a weaned child, perhaps a new level of maturity has begun within me.

The hope of the Gospel is all we ever have. I know that, more deeply now than ever. When all is gone, the "one thing I seek" would be "to dwell in His temple and gaze upon His beauty all the days of my life."

Like the Psalmist, and a weaned child with its' mother, I have to trust that God will answer: by His grace, in His way, in His time, and by His love. I have other questions that should be more important to me. How can I "BE" a well-weaned child of God? And how can I draw my hope from God in these uncertain times? How can I become more of a well-weaned child in these days? How can I learn to become mature, trusting in the goodness of our God to provide in His way and in His time?

Charles Spurgeon, the writer of the book, "The Treasury of David," said of Psalm 131: "It is one of the shortest Psalms to read, but one of the longest to learn." It is a life-long discipline to humble ourselves and quiet our souls to trust in His goodness and promises.

Nowadays, I do not let my mind run wild whenever negative and anxious thoughts creep in, but I rest in the Lord and discipline my mind with the Scriptures to give me hope.

My heart is not proud, O Lord ... It is my prayer for all of us that we will become well-weaned children who choose to quiet our souls in our loving Father's embrace, knowing that He will meet all our needs with good things even in the midst of uncertainties and anxious times.

The Lord indeed is my only, your only, and our only hope both now, and forevermore. O Israel, Hope in the Lord!!!

Paradox is a statement that is seemingly opposed to common sense and yet is perhaps true. In our call to servanthood to our master, we must give up trying to make "sense" and reason with our human minds. Like a well-weaned child in its mother's bosom, trust and leave things that are "too high for me" to our loving and faithful Master and continue to seek Him only to follow His will.

Pray that we will confess with Paul in 2 Corinthian 12 that "when I am weak, I am strong" because "God's power is made perfect in my weakness." May we embrace this paradox of our servanthood and bear true spiritual fruits for His kingdom through His *dunamis* power.

"Through honor and dishonor; through slander and praise; treated as imposters yet we are true; as unknown, and yet well known; as dying, and behold, we live; as sorrowful, yet always rejoicing; as poor, yet making many rich; as having nothing, yet possessing everything" (2 Cor. 6:8-10).

"Therefore, I will boast all the more gladly about my weaknesses, so that Christ's power *dunamis* may rest on me. That is why, for Christ's sake, I delight in weaknesses and insults, in hardships, in persecutions, in difficulties. For when I am weak: I am strong" (2 Cor. 12:9,10).

"One thing I ask from the LORD, this only do I seek: that I may dwell in the house of the LORD all the days of my life, to gaze on the beauty of the LORD and to seek him in his temple." (Psalm 27:4)

(Psalm 27:8) "My heart says of you, 'Seek his face!'
(Psalm 27:8) "Your face, LORD, I will seek."

Chapter Twelve

The Servant in the World

As He is so also are we in the world
(1 John 4:17).

G od is searching for servants whom He can make His leaders in
every area of society. We remember that in the Old Testament,
which contains such rich teaching on what it means to be a servant of
God, God considered all leaders of society to be His servants. Kings,
priests, prophets, musicians, poets, craftsmen, chefs, scholars and
teachers, all were called servants of the Lord. God's Holy Spirit, sometimes called "the Eyes of the Lord," searched for servants, and continues His search today. "For the eyes of the Lord range throughout the
entire earth, to strengthen those whose heart is true to Him" (2 Chron.
16:9 NRSV).

Robert K. Greenleaf, in his prophetic book *Servant Leadership,*
tells us that "the great leader is seen as servant first." He insists that
more servants should emerge as leaders, and that we should follow
only servant-leaders (pp. 7-10).

When more servants become leaders in schools and universities,
banking and mortgage industries, pharmaceutical companies and medicine, in businesses and in arts and entertainment, international law and
local and national governments, and of course in the Church, the world
will become a kinder place. People will find new freedom to grow; the

least privileged in society will benefit. One of my greatest blessings was the privilege of completing my undergraduate study at a "servant led university" (King University, Bristol, Tennessee). The trustees, the president, professors and staff were, and continue to be, servants of God committed to academic and personal excellence, to the glory of God. God plants His servants in every walk of life.

For this reason, the apostle Paul commanded Timothy to encourage his church to lift up prayers of intercession and thanksgiving for all people, especially for "kings and all who are in high positions, that we may lead a peaceful and quiet life, godly and dignified in every way" (1 Tim. 2:1-2). Paul himself continued to pray for God's servants scattered among the churches in the Roman Empire.

We have spoken of how God Himself entered the world as a servant, and by doing so destroyed the power of Satan and brought eternal life to all who will believe and follow Him. He calls all believers to believe in His Son, and to become servants who can become partners with Christ to extend His Kingdom throughout the world. We have emphasized the need to be servants of justice, first to proclaim the justice and righteousness of God in Jesus Christ; but also to change society and transform nations, bringing peace to the world.

When we speak of servants in the world, we remember the young "apostle of Norway" Hans Nielsen Hauge. He knew a great secret that more important and highly placed leaders of his nation did not know. He knew that the only way to change a society is to produce servants who will change it. That is what he did; he trained young men and women in the Word of God and the ways of God and sent them out to every village in Norway. The result was the emergence of Norway as the great nation it is today.

Our task now is to discover some principles that will enable us to bring change to the places where we work; or to the nations we are called to serve. Three simple directions in which we should move will help us along the way.

Go Under

A servant must go under the people he seeks to serve. He practices downward mobility in an upward mobility world. The servant always goes under, beneath the people he serves. Perhaps a personal story will help us understand. My family's first visit to Hawaii was an exciting experience for us all, so much so that our children never wanted to leave. But I had an experience that changed my pattern and philosophy of mission.

We had served as missionaries to Korea for over a decade; but now we needed to be revived. Little did we expect the way God would do it! We went with friends to a lovely beach where we watched people riding the waves as they came to the shore. They used their bodies, without surf boards or other equipment. I thought how nice it would be to body surf. But I didn't know how to enter the ocean into a wave to ride it, so I walked upright directly into the wave, and was knocked for a total flip; fortunately I was not killed. Then a friend showed me the way. "Go under the wave," he said. "Then come up on the other side and ride it in." After a few more failed attempts, I discovered his way actually worked. I dove into the water, underneath the wave, coming up on the backside of the wave and rode it into shore with comfort and ease.

What did I learn? I learned that this is the way a missionary should enter another culture. Go under. Go beneath the people you intend to serve. Take all your gifts and talents and knowledge and money, and dive underneath the wave of that culture. And stay beneath the wave, in the depths of the ocean, until God leads the people of that culture to lift you up and allow you to minister to them.

But this is not a lesson for cross-cultural missionaries only. It is a lesson for God's servants in every walk of society, whether it be the political or diplomatic area, the world of business and economics, education or the arts, or the religious world. A servant must go under the people he or she wishes to serve. This does not mean that we must pretend to be ignorant, or to passively lay aside our educational achievements or talents. It does mean that we must enter every arena of service "in humility, counting others more significant than ourselves" (Phil. 2:3). Jesus came as Lord of all creation, yet He knelt down before His disciples and washed their feet.

Hans Uhrs von Balthasar said it best in his small book *Engagement with God* (Ignatius Press, San Francisco 2008, p. vii). "Since the Church exists to bring the salvation of Christ to all, she must follow Christ's path of 'descent' into the world and assume Christ's form of life. This entails acting and suffering for the sake of 'the least' among us (Mt. 25:40) and bearing responsibility in and with Christ for the destiny of all."

In spite of Jesus' lowering Himself before them, the disciples did not learn this truth until after Jesus was crucified and raised again. Only when the Holy Spirit fell upon them and transformed them did they learn what it means to be a servant of God. Then they laid aside their ambitions and pride, and began to understand that they needed one another as well as the people they served.

Going beneath those we seek to serve involves listening to people and seeking to learn from them. A servant is approachable by the people he serves, at times being willing to be corrected by them. He or she may have more professional knowledge, but not more wisdom. Humility sometimes is born out of humiliation. Going under those we serve is one of the ways God hides us. We become like clay pots that hold a treasure (2 Cor. 4:7), being willing to be broken so that the treasure, Christ in us, may be seen by others. This allows us to see the people we have come to serve and work with as God's gift to us. Then they will invite us to come inside.

Go Inside

I write these words as a cross-cultural missionary, thankful for the great privilege of having been invited to come inside a culture that was far different from mine. To be welcomed as an "insider" rather than an "outsider" is the beginning of all ministry. Both the messenger and the message become genuine and authentic when such identification takes place. (see *Out of the House of Fear Into the House of Love,* David E. Ross, www.ywam.co.kr, 2015)

This principle applies to anyone entering a new place of work, or becoming part of a government or scientific institution. God Himself practiced this strategy. He entered the world by "coming under" humans, as a helpless baby completely dependent on others. He "came inside" by taking on human flesh and identifying with those He came to serve. He was willing to "dive under the wave of human culture" in order to become one with His people. "Since the children have flesh and blood, he too shared in their humanity so that by his death he might break the power of him who holds the power of death – that is, the devil" (Heb. 2:14 NIV). The Son of God's approach was incarnation – going inside and receiving people as His brothers and sisters, His friends.

Openness and transparency are the keys to servants' life together, whether in the church or in the world. Openness to God, but also openness to those with whom we live and work. God will allow us to be community builders in an increasingly isolated world.

Go Alongside

One of the names of the Holy Spirit is *Paraclete;* He comes alongside to strengthen and encourage us; we can do the same by serving those with whom we work by helping them reach their full potential.

You may be entering a new place of employment. You enter as a servant sent by God, both to be blessed by your new work and also to bless those in your workplace. Or you may be planning to move to another nation to serve people there, or to continue your study or research. Wherever you go, and whatever work you may do, you are God's servant.

God will lead you to do three basic things for those to whom you relate. You can go alongside to sustain them by encouraging them through your love and wisdom that God has given you; you can be a small light that points to a Greater Light. You can bring healing to others, and help them overcome their anxieties, loneliness and other weaknesses. And you can believe in them so that they can continue to grow and become better people. Like St. Francis, you can become an instrument of peace wherever you go.

Marks of Our Service in the World

Many years ago, when Ellen and I were preparing to "launch out into the deep" in our ministry, someone handed me a pamphlet that contained the following ideas. I do not remember the exact words, but I was greatly challenged by them. Perhaps they will challenge you also, as you prepare to take the leap of faith into a deeper ministry of the Spirit.

Others may demand authority, that others follow and obey them. You may not. You have the Spirit's authority; it will be recognized when God wants it to be.

Others may set up little kingdoms and measure their success by size, numbers or power. You may not. You are servants of a greater Kingdom.

Others may do ministry for their personal gain. You may not. God delights in your welfare; He will take care of you. The Lord Himself is your Shepherd.

Others may base their ministry on their own strength, power, and knowledge, so that more people will follow them. You may not. You have the strength of the One who raised Jesus Christ from the dead.

Others may go it alone. You may not. You must have *koinonia* fellowship, for accountability and shared ministry.

Others may ignore or hide their character weaknesses and sins, and continue to deceive others. You may not. You are transparent and accountable to those whom you serve.

Others may seek to defend themselves when falsely attacked. You may not. God has promised to defend His servants. But in the midst of these attacks, the Holy Spirit will transform you and fill you with a joy the world can never know.

God has called you to be His servant for such a time as this.

Hymn for Contemplation and Worship

<u>SEE THE SCARS</u> (Is. 53:5; Mark 10:45; 1 John 2:1)

See the scars, feel the pain.
Know the hurting that they know; what's the gain?
Like a winter's driving rain it falls so hard,
and who's to blame?

We who know, we must go;
take the message of the Man of long ago.
Tell the people everywhere:
Look in faith at One who cared.

Chorus:
And you will see the scars,
see the scars of One who died for you.
See the blood that Jesus shed for you.
Take the mercy that He offers you.
O can't you see the scars,
scars that take the sting of death away,
scars that pay what we could never pay,
scars that promise us a better day.
See the scars.

Take a look, take the time,
see behind the frozen eyes the battered minds.
It's a world of desperate need
and will we simply watch them bleed?

(O can't you)
Chorus

On a subway riding into Manhattan from Queens, I tried to express my thoughts once in song—"What would Jesus do on a subway or a train, sitting with the rest in their world's inflicted pain; people running aimlessly, O but nothing is in view? What would Jesus do—through you?"

Our world in these days seems even more troubling and confusing than it was then, almost 40 years ago. We must learn to pay close attention to people's emotional scars today and learn how to meaningfully point them to the life-giving scars of our Savior Jesus Christ.

I wrote this song while ministering to Korean American youth group students in New York City in the mid-1980s. When Holly and I started to work with these young people, it was quite evident that these young people carried enormous burdens and scars living as second generation immigrants caught between two cultures and languages in a very hostile big city environment. First, I wanted them to look to Jesus and see the scars that He bore for them and for all our sakes. Secondly, I also wanted them to see the world around them and see the scars others were bearing and understand their call. "We who know, we must go; Tell the people everywhere: Look in faith at One who cared. We who know, we must go; take the message of the Man of long ago. Tell the people everywhere: 'Look in faith at One who cared.'"

This, I believe, still is the greatest call on the servants of the Lord. We who have known the Scars that brought wholeness to our lives are called to point others to receive hope and wholeness through the scars of Jesus, Lord and Savior.

"But he was pierced for our transgressions, he was crushed for our iniquities; the punishment that brought us peace was on him and by his wounds we are healed" (Is. 53:5).

"For even the Son of Man did not come to be served, but to serve, and to give his life as a ransom for many" (Mark 10:45).

Chapter Thirteen

The Servant's Call

I have called you in righteousness
(Is. 42:6).

Called to be a servant. No one makes the decision easily. We must have childlike faith, but to have such faith in God's steadfast love we must first make a difficult decision. Abraham faced this decision when God called him to leave every human security and follow Him in the direction of an unknown world. What did it mean for him to make this decision? It meant that he must give the Lord a blank check, trusting Him with his whole life. He would be entering a life where he would have to trust in the unseen, hope beyond hope, and break away from the status quo; at the age of seventy-five he would have to go out, *"not knowing where he was going"* (Heb. 11:8).

But Abraham knew, as did young Mary when she was faced with a much greater impossibility, that God is faithful. Faith is trust in God's faithfulness. It is not about accepting dogmas or doctrinal truths about God; nor is it a purely intellectual decision. It is a matter of the heart. Both Abraham and Mary had hearts that were completely open to God, for God was saying to them, as He says to us: "Give me your heart, My son, My daughter; and let your eyes delight in my ways" (Prov. 23:26 NASB). Abraham and Mary became servants of "a captured heart," as David Holdaway says so eloquently in his book *The Captured Heart* (www.lifepublications.org.uk, 2004). He closes his book with this quotation from A.W. Tozer: "The widest thing in the universe is not space, it is the potential of the human heart. Being made in the image of God, it is capable of almost unlimited extension in all directions. And one of the world's greatest tragedies is that we allow our hearts to shrink until there is room in them for little beside ourselves" (p.25).

Just like all the servants in the Bible, we also do not know where our decision to become a servant of the Lord will lead us. But we know the Lord; so we decide, just as Abraham and Mary did, to allow the Lord to "extend" us beyond all human expectations. Our goal is to know God more fully so that we can follow Him in any direction He leads.

The God Who Calls Us to Be His Servant – Is. 42:5-9

God's call to become His servant (Is. 42:5-9) immediately follows the first Suffering Servant Song (Is. 42:1-4). He tells us first what it means to be His servant and what our task will be; then He issues His call. Jesus, who fulfilled Isaiah's prophecy of the Suffering Servant, renews the call by first telling us the cost of following Him and only then gives the call. Jesus calls not only an elite group, His 12 disciples; He calls everyone to follow Him. "Calling the crowd to Him with His disciples, He said to them, 'If anyone would come after me, let him deny himself and take up his cross and follow me" (Mark 8:31).

Who is this God who calls us to become His servants? God is love. He loves us unconditionally and will never forsake us. He surrounds His servants with His loving care. He is infinite in knowledge and wisdom. God's love is all powerful. He reminds us, as He calls us to become His servants, that He is "God, the Lord, who created the heavens and stretched them out, who spread out the earth and what comes from it, who gives breath to the people on it and spirit to those who walk in it" (Is. 42:5). No power of Satan or of humans can touch us without His permission; when we suffer, His love and power sustain us. Job described Him as the One "who can do all things, and no purpose of yours can be thwarted" (Job 42:2). Nothing is impossible with God; He will fulfill all His purposes for His servants. We do what is possible; God does the impossible. God is sovereign, so we can trust Him to fulfill His purposes for our lives as we obey Him.

He is righteous and just. "The Rock! His work is perfect, for all His ways are just; a God of faithfulness and without injustice, righteous and upright is He" (Deut. 32:4 NASB). God is faithful; He will never fail us. He is merciful and forgives us when we sin and restores us when we repent of disobedience.

He is God who chose to identify with humans to such an extent that He became a man, and suffered and died to remove the root of sin in our lives that we might set free. He rose again and sent His Spirit to empower our lives as we serve the world.

He is the God who entered the fiery furnace with three of His servants, and who walked with Daniel in the lions' den. He is our God who invites us to call to Him so that He may tell us great and hidden things that only servants can know, and who empowers His servants to sing songs of praise in the darkest prisons (Jer. 33:1-3; Acts 16:23-25).

God's Promises to His Servants

The Bible is full of promises; casual believers delight in searching for them, but often are unable to enjoy them fully because they fail to see the commands that come with the promises. Of course God's love is unconditional and given to all who will receive it. But most of the covenant promises of provision, protection and wisdom are given only to His servants, who not only rejoice in His promises but also delight in obeying God's commands, and who find their greatest satisfaction in accomplishing the work that He gives us to do. The greatest promise God gives to His servants is to reveal Himself to them, so that they may know the One who is calling them.

God gives three covenant promises to those who respond to His call. "I will take you by the hand and keep you ... I will give you as a covenant for the people, a light for the nations ... New things I now declare; before they spring forth I tell you of them."

"I will take you by the hand and keep you" (Is. 42:6a). God promises His intimacy and protection to His servants. He is both a Father and a Mother to us. "Can a woman forget her nursing child, that she should have no compassion on the son of her womb? Even these may forget, yet I will not forget you. Behold, I have engraved you on the palms of my hands; your walls are continually before me" (Is. 49:15-16). "As one whom his mother comforts, so I will comfort you" (Is. 66:13).

One reason servants of the Lord make their home in the Psalms is because they speak so wonderfully of the love God has for His people and the protection that He offers throughout their lifetime. The Most High God invites His servants to make their home in His secret shelter. It becomes the place both of intimacy and protection. He becomes their refuge and fortress (Ps. 91).

"When you pass through the waters, I will be with you ... when you walk through the fire you shall not be burned" (Is. 43:2). God knows that those who follow His Son will face great dangers from the world and from evil powers. "Fear not, for I am with you; be not dismayed, for I am your God; I will strengthen you, I will help you, I will uphold you with My right hand" (Is. 41:10). "You who have been borne by Me from before your birth, carried from the womb; even to your old age I am He, and to gray hairs I will carry you. I have made, and I will bear; I will carry and will save" (Is. 46:3-4).

"I will give you as a covenant for the people, a light for the nations" (Is. 42:6b-7). God promises to use His servants to bless the world. There are times, when God calls His servants, that He does not grant us a complete understanding of what is involved in following Him, lest we become afraid and turn away. He does give us the promise, but the unfolding of that promise may take place gradually, like the graceful unfolding of a rose as it matures. Perhaps this has been true with your call; it certainly is true of my calling. I was seventeen years old, having just made the life decision of trusting in Jesus Christ and following Him for life, when He spoke to me through these words of Isaiah. This call of God (Is. 42:5-9) has been my life passage since my teenage years; but only now, many decades later, am I discovering the enormous privilege of embodying God's covenant and becoming a light for the nations.

All of God's servants who follow Him as Abraham did—depending on God to lead the way, opening doors and closing others, supplying all his needs, forgiving his sins and correcting His mistakes, hiding him in times of danger, and using him to bless the world—can only stand amazed in His presence and worship Him.

Becoming "a light for the nations" is the specific mission of God's servants. Paul takes these texts from Genesis 12:1-3 and Isaiah 42:5-9 and says that the Lord has commanded him and Barnabas by saying, "I have made you a light for the Gentiles [nations], that you may bring salvation to the ends of the earth" (Acts 13:47). When Jesus Christ gave His promise of the Holy Spirit and His plan for carrying it out, He explained that the mission of His servant Abraham is the same mission His servants have today, to be His witnesses to the whole world. "But you will receive power when the Holy Spirit has come upon you, and you will be My witnesses in Jerusalem and in all Judea and Samaria, and to the end of the earth" (Acts 1:8).

This mission of opening the eyes that are blind and bringing out the prisoners from the dungeons of darkness cannot be carried out in the servant's own power. The Holy Spirit must come upon us like rain on parched and dry ground, to renew and refresh our spirits; like fire, to burn away the destructive sin and useless chaff from our lives, and to empower us to complete His mission.

"Behold, the former things have come to pass, and new things I now declare; before they spring forth I tell you of them" (Is. 42:9).

God promises to speak to His servants of new things that He will do. He spoke to His servant Noah and warned him of His plans to destroy the violence in the world. He spoke to Jeremiah while he was suffering in a dungeon and told him to "call to Me, and I will tell you great and hidden things that you have not known" (Jer. 33:1-3). He gave understanding to Daniel when he was in captivity, so that he could interpret King Nebuchadnezzar's dreams; and later gave him great visions of the coming Kingdom of God. He spoke to Paul and showed him both dangers to avoid and new areas for ministry. He spoke to John while he was in exile on the island of Patmos and revealed the end time events recorded in the book of Revelation.

The question remains. Does God speak to His servants today of "new things before they spring forth?" The answer is both yes and no. Yes! Evidence abounds for God's speaking to His servants today about future events, places to go or not to go, people to meet; things He will do in the servant's life, healings that will surprise medical professionals, or provision for her needs that she would otherwise not expect. God sometimes speaks to His servants of coming revivals, so that both we and others can prepare.

But the answer is no to those who refuse to allow the Word of Christ to dwell richly in them (Col. 3:16), who basically ignore the Bible and speak in ignorance about things to come. A servant who truly desires to know of "new things before they spring forth" will search the Scriptures and listen to the Holy Spirit as He speaks in Scripture as he reads and meditates daily. God will speak to you of new opportunities to witness to the Gospel, or new areas of need around the world of which you may not have been aware. Each morning, allow God to "awaken your ear" to listen as a disciple (Is. 50:4), and ask the Holy Spirit to open your eyes to behold wondrous things in His Word (Ps. 119:18).

Hymn for Contemplation and Worship

<u>Into the Waters Deep</u> (Lk. 5:1-11)
O Simon, on this very day,
put all thy lesser dreams away.
Thine eye cannot a glimpse now see
of all I have in store for thee.
Wilt thou by faith, then, take this leap?
Put out into the waters deep,
and for a catch let down thy net.
My child, thou hast seen nothing yet.

Thy doubtful question well I know:
"Am I to reap where none can sow?"
And weary, too—I see thy strain;
so great the toil, so small the gain.
But hear my words, friend, and obey,
I will transform thy world today,
though thou shalt sense it by degree.
What wonders wait? Obey, and see!

Unworthy dost thou claim to be?
Be wise, My child, and cling to Me.
Hold fast unto My pain-pierced hand.
Upon My merits take thy stand.
To glorify My Name through thee,
shall I restrained, or cautious be?
Behold, My Spirit's untamed pow'r
shall fill thee full for this, thine hour.

Beloved Simon, son of John,
thou shalt catch men from this time on.
And Peter, soon, thy name shalt be

Take up thy cross and follow Me.
Friend, wilt thou also heed Christ's call
to find true life by losing all?
And what is thy new name to be?
If thou wilt dare, obey and see!

This hymn is a meditation on Luke 5:1-11, and was initially written as a poem to be read at the conclusion of a sermon I preached on that passage. Several months after I wrote the poem, I wrote the tune, which I call, DEEP WATERS.

The story of Jesus' dealings with Simon Peter have long been a source of both challenge and encouragement to me. Simon, though full of flaws and often failing, Jesus continues to call him to become Peter. Christ's call on my life is not based on my own gifts or righteousness, but totally on His own merits. He simply asks me to hold on to His "pain-pierced hand" and heed His call. Like Simon, I shall one day become 'Peter' if I will dare to obey. Then, I will surely see what God can do through the one who obeys.

"But whatever were gains to me I now consider loss for the sake of Christ. What is more, I consider everything a loss because of the surpassing worth of knowing Christ Jesus my Lord, for whose sake I have lost all things. I consider them garbage, that I may gain Christ and be found in him, not having a righteousness of my own that comes from the law, but that which is through faith in Christ—the righteousness that comes from God on the basis of faith. I want to know Christ—yes, to know the power of his resurrection and participation in his sufferings, becoming like him in his death, and so, somehow, attaining to the resurrection from the dead. Not that I have already obtained all this, or have already arrived at my goal, but I press on to take hold of that for which Christ Jesus took hold of me" (Phil. 3:7-12

David's Final Word to Servants

You have been chosen and called by God. He has bestowed on you the greatest of gifts: the privilege of working in partnership with His Son, Jesus Christ, as His servant. He has equipped you with His Word, empowered you by His Holy Spirit, and surrounded you with His love.

You will share His ministry of justice for the world; to free people from Satan's injustice to new life in Him, and to free the suffering peoples of the world from the evils brought about by human cruelty and atrocities.

He is your Shepherd, and He will lead you in each step that you take and guide you in directions for ministry that you have never considered before. He has invited you to make your home in the "secret place of the Most High," and to find rest in the shadow of His wings.

You will be tempted, but never beyond what you can bear; He will at that time provide a way out so that you can endure it (1 Cor. 10:13).

You may sometimes become discouraged and want to give up, but God will never give up on you.

You may at times feel frustrated and think that you have labored in vain, but God will continue to bear fruit through you and comfort you by enlarging your vision.

You will suffer, but you will remember when you suffer that you are doing so for Christ's sake. Even though you walk through the valley of the shadow of death, you will not fear; for One walks beside you who is God's Suffering Servant and also His Good Shepherd. He will provide for you all of your needs.

You will never have to walk alone, for God's Spirit has created for you a supernatural *koinonia* community; you will share your life, victories and failures, joys and sorrows, with other servants of the Lord. The outside world will see you and exclaim, "This is amazing! Look how these Christians love one another!"

You will become God's servant of love, to reveal the love of our Father to those who live in darkness. You will be His instruments of peace and healing in a broken world.

There will be times when He hides you to protect you, or to perfect you. Welcome such times, and learn to rejoice in His presence.

Above all, never forget that our Father is waiting to serve you at the Wedding Feast of the Lamb, the end time banquet of Jesus Christ, the victorious Suffering Servant! You have made the decision to heed Christ's call, and He will give you a new name "which no one knows but he or she who receives it" (Rev. 2:17). Remember the closing words of Gary's hymn *Into the Waters Deep,* as God whispers in your ear, "Well done, good and faithful servant. With you I am well pleased."

Friend, wilt thou also heed Christ's call

to find true life by losing all?

And what is thy new name to be?

If thou wilt dare, obey and see!

Gary's Final Word to Servants

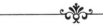

ONESIMUS(Philemon)

Lord, You gave my life to me,
now I give it freely back to You,
my God and King.
For I was useless then,
useless until You laid Your hand
on me, my Healer.

Chorus
So take my life and may I be
useful to Your majesty.
May I reflect Your glory.
As You've loved me, may I love.
As You've touched me, may I touch
with hope and mercy.
I will give my life away.
I will give my life away
(I will find my life in You).

Many times I fail to see
what I was, and what I've come to be
through You, my Friend.
I was a slave before.

I choose to be a slave once more for You,
my Master.

Chorus
(I will find my life in You.)

The song was written while meditating on the slave named Onesimus in the book of Philemon. Onesimus was a slave of Philemon. The name Onesimus was a rather common name for slaves in the Roman Empire of those days as it meant profitable or **useful**. This slave ran away and had become very **useless** to Philemon, his human master.

By God's grace, this runaway slave ran into the Apostle Paul who was under house arrest in Rome, and through Paul's ministry, Onesimus became a follower of Christ. (In tradition Onesimus later himself became a Bishop.)

Here in the book, Paul is pleading to Philemon to receive Onesimus back, saying though he once was "useless" but now he has become "useful."

Martin Luther said that "we are all Onesimuses."

We were all "formerly useless" but God touched us to make us "useful"—true Onesimuses for His majesty, our true master. I wrote the song as a prayer to God to make me more useful.

These days, the song speaks to me in a new and fresh way. After the accident and the injury that took away many of gifts and abilities I felt God had used for His kingdom, I deeply struggled with my "usefulness." I didn't know what I can do to make myself "useful" when I had to depend upon others for everything. I used to consider teaching, speaking and writing to be my spiritual gifts and when I used them I felt useful and that I was doing God's work. When those were stripped away I felt so useless and went into a deep depression which led to a mental breakdown.

It has nearly been 12 years since the accident, and slowly but surely God's faithful leading and healing has brought me to a point where I am learning afresh what it means to be a servant who is "useful" for His majesty. I don't have the position or platform for ministry anymore. Neither do I have abilities like I used to have. But I am learning that my usefulness as His servant is not measured by how others or I view them. God sees my willingness and obedience to seemingly smaller and lesser servant roles in my daily life with my family and others. My prayer is same as when I first wrote the song; I want to be "Onesimus" for His majesty by choosing to be His bond-slave once more and daily reflect His glory to others.

Dear fellow servants of our Lord, do you also truly want to be "useful—Onesimus" for His Majesty? Choose to be His slave once more; reflect His glory by loving others as He has loved you, touch others as He has touched you; and give your life away ... then, you will surely find your life in Him.

Appendix 1

Hymns & Meditations/Hymn Links and Guitar Chords

You can find all these songs on Gary's YouTube channel (gap2Theos) in the playlist linked here: https://tinyurl.com/theheartofaservant

His POIEMA! (Ephesians)
See the words and comments at the end of Chapter 1
Text and Tune: gap2Theos (2013-15) Tune: WE PROCLAIM HIM!

The Righteous One
See the words and comments at the end of Chapter 2
Text and Tune: gap2Theos (2010)

Jesus is LORD!
See the words and comments at the end of Chapter 3
Text and Tune—gap2Theos (1983? 2020)

The Spirit of the Lord
See the words and comments at the end of Chapter 4.
Text: gap2Theos (2005) Tune: WONDROUS LOVE

Rule in This Place
See the words and comments at the end of Chapter 5.
Text and tune: gap2Theos (1988?)

Wondrous Love
See the words and comments at the end of Chapter 6.
Text and Tune: gap2Theos (2010; 14) / Tune: TRIUNE BLISS

The Wall Brought Down
See the words and comments at the end of Chapter 7.
Text and Tune: gap2Theos (2010; 14) / Tune: BROKEN WALL

To Hear as Those Well Taught
See the words and comments at the end of Chapter 8.
The Tune is called KINGSFOLD.

Holy Communion / koinonia (κοινωνία)
See the words and comments at the end of Chapter 9.
Text & tune κοινωνία/KOINONIA:
gap2Theos & George MacDonald (2016, 22)

Follow Your Lord
See the words and comments at the end of Chapter 10.
Text and tune: gap2Theos (1983)

Like a Well-Weaned Child / Psalm 131
See the words and comments at the end of Chapter 11.
Text and Tune: gap2Theos (1996)

SEE THE SCARS
See the words and comments at the end of Chapter 12.
Text and Tune: gap2Theos (1986)

Into the Waters Deep

See the words and comments at the end of Chapter 13.
Text: gap2Theos (2006) Tune: DEEP WATERS

ONESIMUS (Philemon)

See the words and comments after my final thoughts.
Text & Tune: gap2Theos (1993)

My CCLI Copyright number for these songs is
CAT26863

Appendix 2

Recommended Reading
for St. Francis of Assisi

G. K. Chesterton, Saint Francis of Assisi (Brewster, MA: Paraclete Press, 2009)

Duane Arnold and George Fry, Francis, A Call to Conversion (Grand Rapids, MI: Zondervan Publishing House, 1988)

Saint Bonaventure, The Life of St. Francis of Assisi (Gastonia, NC: Tan Books, 2010)

Augustine Thomas, O.P., Francis of Assisi, A New Biography (Ithaca, NY: Cornell University Press, 2012)

Omer Englebert, Saint Francis of Assisi (Ann Arbor, MI: Servant Books, 1965)

Jon M. Sweeney, The St. Francis Prayer Book (Brewster, MA: Paraclete Press, 2004)

Jon M. Sweeney, Translator, Francis of Assisi, The Essential Writings– In His Own Words (Brewster, MA: Paraclete Press, 2018)

CPSIA information can be obtained
at www.ICGtesting.com
Printed in the USA
BVHW081623240922
647685BV00001B/8